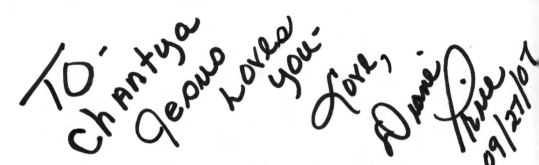

To: Chantya
Jesus loved you.
Love,
Diane Price
09/27/07

PRAYING

THROUGH

SORROWS

DUTCH S*HEETS*
—and—
CHRIS J*ACKSON*

Destiny Image® Publishers, Inc.

P.O. Box 310

Shippensburg, PA 17257-0310

*"Speaking to the Purposes of God for This Generation
and for the Generations to Come"*

ISBN 0-7684-2254-X

For Worldwide Distribution
Printed in the U.S.A.

This book and all other Destiny Image, Revival Press, MercyPlace,
Fresh Bread, Destiny Image Fiction, and Treasure House books are available
at Christian bookstores and distributors worldwide.

1 2 3 4 5 6 7 8 9 10 / 10 09 08 07 06 05

For a U.S. bookstore nearest you, call
1-800-722-6774.

For more information on foreign distributors, call
717-532-3040.

Or reach us on the Internet:

www.destinyimage.com

Dedication

For Alexis

Endorsements

With poetic words of beauty and biblical clarity, *Praying Through Sorrows* draws you into the heart of God, gives you a much needed perspective of pain and suffering, then equips you to "live again." This book is a must read for those desiring the eternal vantage on hardships and the privileged intimacy with Christ that only comes through suffering.

Norm Willis
Senior Pastor of Christ Church Kirkland
Author, Speaker

Loss is a part of life; how we process loss and reflect faith in the midst of our grief is one of the keys to life. In *Praying Through Sorrows* Chris Jackson and Dutch Sheets give us great wisdom and knowledge on experiencing the presence of God in the midst of loss and sorrow. In this book they ask a question, "Will you be made whole?" This is the time where our future is being determined. If we allow grief to settle in our spirit, then we will never have the strength to grab hold of the best that God has for us ahead. *Praying through Sorrows* will encourage you to press through your grief and past your loss into a new dimension of joy.

Dr. Chuck D. Pierce
President, Glory of Zion International Ministries, Inc.
Vice President, Global Harvest Ministries
Apostolic Director, United State Strategic Prayer Network

Praying Through Sorrows touches the heart of each of us who has lost a loved one. Through personal experience and biblical evaluation, Chris Jackson and Dutch Sheets explore the foundation of individual tragedy. Mr. Jackson opens his own heart to us and allows us to feel his personal pain, suffering, confusion, and triumphs in life. His candidness and honesty are refreshing and allow readers to investigate their own personal life stories with a new perspective.

Michael Sedler
Author, Speaker

Chris Jackson has weathered tragedy and sorrow while ultimately strengthening his family and gaining a closer walk in Jesus Christ. *Praying Through Sorrows* is a roadmap for everyone, directing us to preserve and grow through situations that might otherwise destroy the joy that God intends for all of us.

Judge Philip J. Van de Veer

New hope, courage, and strength flow from the pages of this book to those who have experienced deep pain, tragedy, or heartache. Pastor Chris Jackson shares the heart-wrenching story of his family's loss and asks the difficult questions of life. The biblical answers are amazing and reveal insight for those in even the most hurtful of circumstances. Very readable, sensitive, and original!

Dr. Stan Fleming
Gate Breaker Ministries
Author, Pastor

Have you ever known grief? Has it ever seemed almost unbearable? If so, Chris Jackson and Dutch Sheets will convince you that there is hope. Real hope! Your sorrow can be turned into joy as you read the pages of this wonderful book, *Praying Through Sorrows*.

C. Peter Wagner, Chancellor
Wagner Leadership Institute

Table of Contents

Introduction

"*P*ursue, for you shall surely overtake them and without fail, recover all.*" With these words, my world began to unravel. I was sitting in a straight-backed hospital chair when I read them. The beautiful wife of my youth lay sleeping beside me, recovering from an evening of hard labor. Nine months pregnant, exhausted, and clothed in her pastel hospital gown, she appeared to me lovelier than I dare describe. Unbidden, the words of a love poem flooded my memory:

> *To rid my world of its darkest night*
> *A maid from heaven was sent,*
> *An oracle of purest light*
> *Thank God, to me, her gifts were lent.*

She lay, stealing more of my heart with every breath. Thanking God for blessing me far beyond my worth, I relaxed slightly in the stiff chair, grateful for a moment's reprieve. Jessica had gone into labor 15 hours earlier, but had progressed so slowly that she had been given the night to rest in anticipation of an early morning delivery of our first beautiful baby. In those sacred moments of silence without the kind concern of nurses and family members, I read these words of the Lord to the pre-king David at Ziklag: *"Pursue, for you shall surely overtake them and without fail, recover all."* It was the late evening of May 13, 1996, and as I read these words, empathizing with the heartbroken

9

David, I knew this text would produce a glorious sermon of inspiration and encouragement for the people of God. As I savored the Lord's presence and the stillness of the moment, I never dreamed that these words would become my lifeline. On May 13, First Samuel 30 was the text of my next sermon. On May 14, it became a word of the Lord to which I would desperately cling for the next three-and-a-half years. Today, nearly eight years later, the words haunt me. I have never preached this sermon, but I have lived it one thousand times. *"Pursue, for you shall surely overtake them and without fail recover all."*

On May 14, 1996, after 30 hours of labor and an emergency c-section, our first daughter was born. At 6 pounds, 4 ounces and 18.5 inches long, Alexis Grace was beautiful. She had the brilliant blue eyes and curly hair of her mother. Never did we dream we could bond so quickly. Never did we dream how fiercely and deeply parental love could flow. Never did we dream of such horror as we faced those first few hours, nights, weeks, months, and years.

Upon her birth, sweet Alexis entered a world of suffering. Something had gone wrong. She wasn't breathing, and as they feverishly worked to achieve resuscitation, the color drained from our world.

The first time I touched her was in the neo-natal intensive care unit. Breathing on a respirator, she lay in the incubator, a tiny, exposed carrier of my heart. I stooped to kiss her right knee and as my lips touched the softness of her newborn skin, raw emotion ripped upward from the floor and enveloped my soul in pain.

The NICU is a pretty good place to cry. A tender nurse pressed a cloth diaper into my hand as she left me alone in the shadows with my darling baby girl. I wept for an hour as Alexis held tenuously to life and Jessica recovered from her surgery. There, amidst the ragged sobs of exhaustion, grief, and fear, the words enveloped me again. *"Pursue, for you shall surely overtake them and without fail recover all."*

Eight years ago as a weeping, young father, I had no fore-knowledge of the road we would be asked to walk. I had no idea it would take us into seven surgeries and dozens of hospitalizations. I had no idea it would be a rapid descent into despair. I had no knowledge of how deeply a father's and mother's heart could grieve. There, in the dimly lit intensive care unit, all I knew was that I loved Alexis, that her grip on life was frail, and that God had spoken to me: "Pursue!"

Between the promise of recovery and the completed miracle lies a vast graveyard of Christian faith, and, for at least a portion of their lifetimes, the majority of Christendom lives there. Waiting for breakthrough, believing for the promises, and looking to the appointed hope, they struggle to stay the course. This book is intended to be a spiritual ambu bag that pumps fresh life into those living residents of spiritual graveyards.

In Matthew 10:6, Jesus said to His disciples, *"Go rather to the lost sheep of the house of Israel."* In the Greek language of New Testament writing, the word *lost* literally means to be destroyed, either temporally or eternally. There are destroyed people in the family of God. Will their destruction be temporal or eternal? Who will minister to them? Jesus continues in the next verse saying, *"Preach, saying, 'The kingdom of heaven is at hand.'"* *Kingdom* literally means the royal dominion of the king and the phrase *at hand* means to come near the desired and cherished fellowship (with Him). It means that the king, in all His royal dominion, desires to draw near to the destroyed people of His Kingdom. He desires *you!*

Four years ago, Alexis died in my arms. Since her death, I've experienced more pain than I knew the human soul could bear. My heart has splintered a thousand times. I've cried in the fetal position. I've sobbed and cursed, and I've wanted to die.

I've also lived again. The Lord hasn't answered all my questions, but I can see Him holding on to my loose ends. I didn't always see Him there, and you may not either. That's okay.

There's a little phrase in Genesis that occurs after the sin and fall of Adam and Eve. It says "...Adam lived." This Hebrew word for *lived* means to live again. Adam lived and died in Eden, and then he began to live again. Oh, precious sons and daughters and mothers and fathers! You, who have shuddered with loss and grief, I promise you that, as Adam did, you will live again.

Please join me in evaluating the biblical response to pain, tragedy, and loss. It might be different than what you have been told. You might experience the freedom to be real. Indulge me as I share my story. Open your heart and allow the lover of your soul to revive you.

1

Loose Ends

So my pursuit began! From day one of her life, I fought for Alexis' miracle.

With all my might, I pursued the word of the Lord for my beautiful daughter. Remember our Scripture? *"Pursue, for you shall surely overtake them and without fail recover all."* I pursued so I could recover. I didn't know I could run so fast in pursuit. I didn't know I could fight so hard or pray so fervently or memorize so much Scripture or believe God in the face of such hell. Please hear my heart! There is no boasting as I relay the story of my pursuit—I merely did what any desperate father would do. I shouldn't be surprised at the intensity of my pursuit. After all, it's astounding what the love of a husband and father can produce in a man. Jacob worked seven years for Rachel, and they seemed but a few days for his love for her. David pursued the Amalekites at Ziklag and crushed their army of far superior numbers. Simeon and Levi (although cursed for their cruelty) slew an entire city for the revenge of their shamed sister.

I pursued from the moment she was born.

I pursued as the negative reports began flooding in.

I pursued when she wouldn't take a bottle and we were forced to surgically insert a feeding tube into her stomach. I pursued when this surgery was ineffective and two additional surgeries were required to complete the task.

I pursued when a panel of pediatric specialists informed us that she probably wouldn't live beyond her first year.

I pursued until the first seven weeks of her life were complete and we were finally allowed to bring her home from the NICU.

I studied and memorized every Hebrew and Greek Scripture reference to divine healing, and I pursued amidst my tears.

I pursued when they informed us that she couldn't see.

I continued my pursuit when we discovered her seizure disorder and the neurologist was at a loss for a diagnosis.

A bitter day of pursuit came the first time I had to administer CPR to her. Jessica and I were conducting a young adult church service in a park on a lovely summer day when Alexis stopped breathing during the sermon. A young nursing student walked me through the steps of mouth-to-mouth resuscitation. In God's providence and love, it happened that a dear family friend who worked as a paramedic was patrolling the park that day, and he arrived within minutes to assist and transport little Alexis to the hospital.

I really tried hard to pursue when, at five months old, after dozens of resuscitations, performed by me and Jessica, we submitted to the doctor's request to perform a tracheotomy. This shocking, heart-wrenching procedure increased her breathing efficiency and reduced the need for the drastic measures of CPR and mouth-to-mouth resuscitation, but it also precipitated the need for 24-hour nursing care in our home. My sweet wife insisted on being personally trained and performing Alexis' primary care during the day while the nurses moved into our home for the night watches.

Despite all this, the Lord really did help me to pursue.

From Jamaica to Canada, Alexis was on prayer chains. The prayers lifted for her little life must have overwhelmed the angels responsible for catching our prayers and adding them to the bowls near the altar of Heaven (see Rev. 8:3). Alexis taught me to pray. She taught me to pursue. When I was too weak to pursue, our church pursued for us. I never regretted a minute of pursuit.

I pursued through scoliosis.

I pursued through sessions with respiratory, physical, nutrition, and vision specialists, osteopaths, neurologists, family doctors, and home health care agencies.

I pursued through hip surgery.

I pursued through a dozen bouts with pneumonia.

I pursued through an oral surgery that left her gums blackened and scarred.

I pursued when her perfectly healthy baby sister, Amber Hope, was born.

I pursued through fatigue, grief, and despair.

I pursued until I believed the word.

I pursued until I knew the Lord would heal her.

I pursued until I trusted that the Lord knew best.

I pursued on August 26, 1999, when she died in my arms. Jessica looked at me minutes before her death and said, "You know, she was never really ours." As I nodded through my tears, she spoke again, "No regrets." I really did pursue, and on September 1, I preached her memorial service with no regrets. I shared from Hebrews 13:1 on the concept of entertaining *"angels unawares"* (see KJV). Oh, she most certainly was an angel! She was my angel.

We fought a good fight! Alexis was a champion. She endured more in her three-and-a-half years than any person should ever be forced to bear. I'm glad she's with Jesus now. I'm truly glad that she'll never have her heart broken or skin a knee or suffer betrayal or rejection or loss. At the end, I was glad the Lord took her home. I'm glad she's in Heaven, but I'm now left with a problem. She took my heart with her. You see, although I pursued with every fiber of my being, she was never my project. She was my baby, and I loved her with the love that only a desperate, warring father can know.

She was my daughter. I sang to her (our favorite was the love song from Snow White). I combed her long, beautiful, amber-colored hair. I danced with her (our favorite dancing song was a duet by Celine Dion and Luciano Pavarotti). Jessica and I read her stories, celebrated her birthday parties, used her special stroller in the park, took dozens of photographs, dedicated her to God in a special baby dedication service, and loved her fiercely.

I am so happy for Alexis! She's living our promised inheritance. She'll be my heavenly tour guide some day. I can't wait for that day, but here, today, I'm still a young man with a lot of life left to live; and although our fight ended in her victory (I'm just sure that all of Heaven stood in respectful ovation as she came home), I'm not quite sure how to live without her.

I'm so happy that she can finally see. She's beheld over three years of splendor now. She's seen colors my mind has no capacity to imagine. She's seen Jesus in ways that I only long to see Him. She can see. I'm so happy, and yet my problem persists; because when her gorgeous, blue eyes were eternally healed, mine went dim. I'm having trouble seeing clearly. You see, although I really do have perspective, there's this loose end that now dangles from my Christian faith and threatens to blind me. What do I do with the memory of Alexis? What do I do with my experience of pursuit? Oh, I know, someday I'll be able to help people, and I really do desire to minister from my time with her—but what about my heart? What about Jessica? What about little Amber Hope who lost her big sister when she was only six months old? God doesn't owe me. I'm not mad at Him (although He's certainly big enough to handle my pain and anger and humanity), but I do need help. In fact, if He doesn't help me, I might not make it—even after a valiant pursuit.

What do you do with a loose end? Most of us have them. Yours may not involve a child, but you've probably experienced a paradox. Your prayer may not have been answered when you just knew it should have been. There are many promises that have yet to be fulfilled. There may be some that look as if they'll never be fulfilled. Divorce, suicide, loss, prodigal children, sudden unemployment…oh, the list goes on. What do we, the sons and daughters of God, the ransomed and redeemed, do with our loose ends? Do we give them a good tug and wait to see how much of our life unravels? Do we cut the loose end off? Some people do. Some people cut off the loose end and pretend it never existed. Your loose end exists! Faith is never blind. Faith is based on the reality of a word from God. We can't ignore the realities of loss and grief, but what do we do with them?

Could it be possible that what today is a loose end is actually the first thread of a future anchor? Maybe someday this ugly, loose end will connect with another loose end that has dangled in my path, and they will form an anchor that will secure the fabric of my life. Perhaps what was meant for evil will someday be used for good. These words are true, but I hesitate as I write them. Well-intentioned friends and loved ones tried to share the truth of these words with us prematurely. Someone encouraged my wife's faith and said, "You really are a saint." She replied, "I wanted to be a mother, not a saint."

I know what Romans 8:28 says. I know that Paul said, *"All things work together for good,"* but I also know that this is a wisdom verse, a perspective verse. It is not a verse designed to be healing ointment for the newly bruised soul. All things *will* work together for good in time. The sum total of your experiences, when it's all said and done, will have produced a synergistic effect of good.

God is good. God is good where you are concerned, and yet you still have your loose ends. For a long time, I felt like my loose end was strangling me.

The Anatomy of Grief

I thought I had everything buttoned up. My life was planned, and my call from God was secure. I had married a fairy-tale princess, and God was good. My goals were set for the next 50 years, and I had nothing left to do but follow Jesus and change the world. I had a lot of answers and a lot of vision for my life. I never dreamed that one season of freakish tragedy could change so much.

When Jessica and I left our wedding reception, we were driven into the sunset in a pink Cadillac, and I knew we were graced by God.

On the beaches of Hawaii, I sensed we were destined for paradise.

When Jessica conceived Alexis, I knew that God had strategically planned the timing of our first child and that this baby was born for great things.

When Jessica was terribly ill with morning sickness for nine months straight, I knew that it was worth it.

When Alexis was born with brain damage, I knew that God was the healer.

I knew it three years later when we were still fighting.

After she died, I knew very little.

I knew I loved Jessica. I knew I loved Amber. I knew I was still a Christian, but beyond that, I wasn't sure. No one ever told me that grief would turn me into the question man.

Who am I now?

How can I hurt this badly and ever hope to live again?

What's wrong with me?

What now?

And, of course, why?

Your experience certainly varies from mine, but you have probably faced (or are facing) some of the same questions. They can haunt us.

Who Am I Now?

When Alexis was alive, at least I had a cause. Although hurting deeply and profoundly, at least I was the fighting father. I knew exactly which Scriptures to stand on and which books to read. I knew how to pray, and I knew the right confession to speak. Unwittingly, she became my identity. I was Alexis' dad.

I was so sure of myself before the loss; but when she died, a part of me died too. The problem is that no one told my head or my heart. I still wanted to check on her in the night. I thought for sure she would still need me. Children aren't supposed to die before their parents. It isn't right.

I felt robbed. We were supposed to take her to preschool and teach her to play soccer. I had already begun to pray that she would find the right husband. I was supposed to walk her down the aisle someday.

Who am I now? I'm still her dad, but it will never be the same. She's with her *heavenly* Father now.

Our third daughter, Madelyn Joy, is one year old now. I don't like saying I have three daughters, but I hate saying that I have only two.

I love talking about her, but as soon as I do, I regret it. No one understands. I know they try to, but they can't. Well…some people can. However, those who have shouldered the unthinkable don't say much. They just listen. They just love. They've had to rediscover who they are too.

19

How Can I Hurt This Badly and Ever Hope to Live Again?

"Is Alexis ever coming back?" Amber asked this question the other day on our way home from preschool. I smiled and did my best to explain Heaven to a four year old. She probably understands it better than I do. She asked, "Does Jesus have lots of toys? Can Alexis fly in Heaven?"

Amber talks about her all the time now. I'm not sure if she actually remembers Alexis or if she just sees the photos of the two of them and wonders.

Since Alexis' health was fragile from birth and we courted death on many occasions, some of our friends thought we would be more prepared for losing her. They thought the grief we faced during her brief life would count towards the pain of her death. Maybe it did. I don't know if you can quantify pain and grief like that. All I know is that when she died in my arms, I felt my soul shatter.

There have been times, too numerous to count, when choking waves of sorrow have threatened to capsize my life. Then someone would say her name: "I miss Alexis." My breath would catch, my throat would constrict, the tears would mock my attempt to stop them, and the tidal wave of grief would rise again. I didn't know the human heart could endure such pain and continue beating. I certainly didn't think it could heal again.

What's Wrong With Me?

It's a fair question to ask because everything feels so wrong after a tragic loss.

I felt so very alone. I didn't realize that everyone who emerges from the trauma of shattered dreams feels so alone. I didn't realize that the survivors of the catastrophic loss of a loved one or a marriage or a dream feel vulnerable and conspicuous and like they're stuck in suspended animation. Life moves on for the rest of the world, but it seems to stop for the grieving. Randy Becton in *Everyday Comfort* described it this way:

> Frequent periods of anxiety are normal because of the separation caused by death. Numbness, emptiness, loneliness and isolation can make even normal tasks such as doing the laundry, grocery shopping and vacuuming seem impossible to accomplish. Grief can erupt at awkward moments: at lunch, singing in church, starting your car. Don't be ashamed when your grief does not follow a normal timetable. Periods of anger toward your loved one, other members of the family, yourself, or God are normal. Watch out for nighttime. Listen to Job: *"My bones are pierced in me at night, and my gnawing pains take no rest"* (Job 30:17).[1]

I often felt a panicky fear akin to paranoia. I couldn't explain it.

I wonder if I was as conspicuous as I felt? I was just certain that everyone was staring at me.

I love her cemetery, and I hate it with every cell of my being. I hate going, and I dread leaving.

It was blisteringly hot in August when she died, and yet I could never get warm.

Grief is unnerving. It's too quiet. Randy Becton went on to write:

> C.S. Lewis's honesty about his grief gives me courage and hope for mine. His *A Grief Observed* has helped those to whom I have recommended it. His line "I not only live each day in grief, but live each day thinking about living each day in grief" underscores the fresh fatigue grief often brings.
>
> Like the indoor jogger on a treadmill, the painful loss runs in place over and over again. The thought, Will it

ever be different? sinks the heart in fear. It is true that you will not "get over it"; it will always matter. But it will not always be a searing iron burning your spirit. The good news is that the pain will take its place in the heart's memory chamber as sweet sadness.[2]

What Now?

She's gone. I know it, but I still can't believe it. I miss her so badly that at times I fear I'm being swallowed up in endless sorrow. Where do I go from here?

And, of course, *why*?

Did I really hear from God in the NICU on the day of her birth?

Did I miss Him?

If I missed Him, how can I trust the other things I thought He told me?

If I heard Him correctly, then why didn't I receive a miracle when I was just certain that He had told me to fight for one?

If He didn't come through for me *then*, how can I trust Him *now*?

Is the sovereignty of God merely a cop-out?

Why do bad things happen to good people?

How should I then live?

Eight years after my questioning began, I haven't found many answers, but I have found Him. Jesus doesn't have all the answers; He is the answer. Maybe He will make sense of your loose ends in this lifetime, and maybe He won't. The one constant is Him. He will be there (even if you don't feel His presence right now).

Someday, your loose end will be gently reconnected. John Yates in *Leadership Journal* related a story of reconnecting:

The only survivor of a shipwreck washed up on a small uninhabited island. He cried out to God to save him, and every day he scanned the horizon for help, but none seemed forthcoming.

Exhausted, he eventually managed to build a rough hut and put his few possessions in it. But then one day, after hunting for food, he arrived home to find his little hut in flames, the smoke rolling up to the sky. The worst had happened; he was stung with grief.

Early the next day, though, a ship drew near the island and rescued him.

"How did you know I was here?" he asked the crew.

"We saw your smoke signal," they replied.

Though it may not seem so now, your present difficulty may be instrumental to your future happiness.[3]

I'm not trying to be flippant about your pain or offer a pat answer to your shattered soul's questions. I'm sharing truth. The passion of God is to wrap His heart around hurting humanity, hear their cry, and restore their dreams. In fact, let me prove this to you in the next chapter.

2

Why Are You Crying?

She wept. She had tried to conceal her sniffles and muffled sobs, but she was about to drown in her sorrow.

She wept. The cry began as a choking gasp and ended as a heartrending wail that echoed the tearing pain of her soul. Oh, how she wept!

She cried and cried and then the real crying began. Oh, Mary, I wish I could comfort you in your grief!

Her day began before dawn while it was still quite dark. Wrapped in her thick shawl, she felt the morning chill clinging, it seemed, to the very marrow of her bones. It was cold. Her heart felt as if it had frozen over.

She had never experienced this type of pain before. It hadn't hurt this badly when the people had called her a whore. Even the abuse she had experienced at the hands of the sinful men who lusted for her and then despised her didn't hurt like this. She had lived her share of rejection and betrayal and loss. She had spent many nights alone with her tears. How could this feel so much worse? How could she ever hurt so thoroughly and deeply and hope to survive? She wondered if she might die right there in the garden. Death seemed a welcome alternative to this great pain.

Her chest hurt. Although her grief was internal, the very act of breathing was excruciating. She feared that the effort to draw her breath in between her shrieks and sobs would undo her. Her stomach was coiled in steel knots. Her legs were weak and shaky. She felt sweat on her forehead and a feverish dizziness infected her veins. She was so cold.

The sun was beginning to rise in the east. The day slowly dawned, and the silvery sheen of morning began to wrestle with the blackness of night for dominance of the skies. The thought of another day was ghastly. She had lived two days since His death, and the sorrow was only intensifying. Especially today. Someone had taken His body.

What horror it was to arrive at His tomb for a time of mourning only to find that someone had desecrated the grave and confiscated the body. Who would do such a thing? It almost didn't matter. It just hurt so badly.

The sky was rapidly growing brighter, but the flow of her tears only quickened. "Oh, how I miss You!" she shouted to the skies and then collapsed on the garden floor in a sobbing, shuddering heap.

Get up, Mary! I can't stand to watch you like this. You're reminding me too much of me in the "Garden for Faith and Healing" outside Sacred Heart Medical Center in Spokane, Washington. It was the morning after, and I had awakened the dawn with my tears. I thought my chest might explode, and I honestly feared that the pain would kill me. No words of comfort in the world could have saved me then. Mary, I'm sure you felt the same way...

...until He spoke to you.

He was only a gardener and His question seemed so odd considering that you were weeping outside a tomb. He asked you, "Why are you crying?" The question could have seemed so insensitive since you were lying prostrate before the mouth of the newly used grave.

"Why am I crying?" you thought. "Don't you have any idea what happened this weekend? Don't you know whose grave this is? Oh, do you know who has taken Him? Do you know where they have taken Him? Please, Sir, tell me where they have taken Him, and I will go and take Him back.

"Why am I crying? Only because I feel that my heart has just died and yet I must continue to live for another thirty years.

"Why am I crying? I'm crying because He was the only person to ever love me. No, I don't mean in a romantic sense. I mean in a God-sense. He just loved me. I did nothing for Him. I didn't deserve His love. In fact, when He found me, He had to cast seven devils out of me to even have a coherent conversation with me. He healed me. I was mean. I was hateful and cruel. Deeply abused, I was abusive to those around me. I so desperately wanted to be loved, and when He found me, I found life. He was my Savior.

"Why am I crying? Did you know they killed Him two days ago? They crucified Him on a Roman cross. I watched until I couldn't stand it. I vomited. I wept. I cursed. I wanted to die. I miss Him. Yes, I could cry for a lot of reasons, but mostly I'm crying because I just miss Him. My heart aches without Him.

"Why am I crying? I don't know what else to do.

"By the way, you are the gardener here, aren't you?"

Oh Mary, if you only knew the implications of His question and who it was who asked it!

Let's leave Mary standing before the supposed gardener for a few moments and consider the incredible significance of this encounter. There were 15 appearances to individuals or groups of individuals by Jesus Christ listed in the New Testament after His resurrection from the dead. Each appearance is rich in insight and revelation; however, His first appearance probably reveals more of His compassionate heart than any of the others that followed. The first time we see Him after His resurrection reveals a staggering truth, but in order to catch the full weight of that truth, we must evaluate the timing of this first sighting.

The resurrection of Jesus Christ from the dead is, far and away, the greatest event in the history of mankind. There has never been, nor will there ever be, anything as significant as the resurrection. On the validity of this one event hangs all of Christianity. Our faith in the resurrection of Jesus from the dead is more important than our belief in any other theological issue.

The resurrection is not just one of the miracles that Jesus performed on earth. It wasn't a sign and a wonder right up there with turning water into wine or walking on water or healing a blind man. Christianity rises or falls based on whether or not Jesus was physically raised from the dead. This fantastic event is either a cruel, merciless hoax that has left us all deceived, or it is true. If it is true, the subsequent implications are tremendous.

If Jesus was a liar, then He was defeated on a wooden cross 2,000 years ago and we are tragically deceived. However, if He truly was God in the flesh, and if He was raised from the dead to emerge victorious from the tomb and reopen personal access to a relationship with God the Father, then that means I can trust Him. That would mean that I can build my life on His teachings. If He had power over death, hell, and the grave, then surely He can heal the pain of my loss. If He rose from the dead, like He said He would do, then I can trust His other promises. Do you remember some of those other promises?

To be absent from the body [is] to be present with the Lord (2 Corinthians 5:8).

Do not grieve as those who have no hope [implying that we have a hope] (see 1 Thessalonians 4:13).

Precious in the sight of the Lord is the death of His saints (Psalm 116:15).

Nothing can separate us from the love of Christ [not even our grief] (see Romans 8:39).

Blessed are the dead who die in the Lord...they [have ceased] *from their labors* (Revelation 14:13).

Without taking the time here to give a thorough defense for the resurrection of Jesus, let me quote Josh McDowell and state that it is an irrefutable fact that validates all the other claims of Christ. McDowell wrote in *The New Evidence That Demands a Verdict:*

After more than seven hundred hours of studying this subject and thoroughly investigating its foundation, I have come to the conclusion that the resurrection of Jesus Christ is one of the most wicked, vicious, heartless hoaxes ever foisted upon the minds of men, OR it is the most fantastic fact of history.[4]

This fantastic event *did* occur, and John captured the first subsequent appearance and spoken words of Jesus. Don't you think that Jesus' first few comments on the heels of this defining moment of mankind would be steeped in profound significance? Notice with me what Jesus did *not* say.

He didn't say, "Where is Pontius Pilate? It's payback time."

He didn't say, "Thank you" to the angels for rolling back the stone for Him.

As far as we know, He didn't take a few moments to speak with the Father.

He didn't round up the elders and priests who opposed Him to teach them a lesson. By the way, it's so sad that the priests who had Him crucified never saw Him again on planet Earth. Of the 15 appearances of Jesus after the resurrection, none of them were to the priests or religious leaders.

On the heels of this moment that had been planned since the foundation of the world, on the heels of brutalization by Roman guards, on the heels of death on a cross, on the heels of the resurrection from the dead, Jesus says to *Mary*: "Why are you crying?" and "Who are you looking for?"

Why are you crying? Jesus, the resurrection Himself, has a burning question for humanity. "Why are you crying?" He says, "Oh, please don't make Me use My omniscience for this one. I just want you to confide in Me. Why are you crying *today*? What's hurting your heart *today*?"

When Jesus asked this question of Mary, He used a word for *crying* that meant to sob and wail versus a quiet sniffling. He asked, "Why are you wracked in grief and shaken by sorrow?"

The heart of humanity contains a cry.

John's account tells us that Mary thought He was a gardener! This wasn't because Jesus was so plain and nondescript. She thought He was a gardener because He wanted to send a message to mankind: "I've just destroyed death. I *am* the resurrection and the life. I am the creator of the cosmos and I'm just like a gardener. I care about individual flowers. Mary, why are you crying? Mary, it looks like life has torn off some of your petals. I want you to think of Me as a tender husbandman who delights to revive wilting gardens."

Jesus is asking this question of you today. No, He's not making small talk. He isn't merely being polite. He's not trying to psychoanalyze you. He just wants to know: Why are you crying? You see, He's timeless. For Him, He feels as if He's just risen from the dead, and He desperately wants to share some resurrection life and power. He asks, "Why are you crying?" and "Who are you looking for?"

That's another great question. Notice He says, "who" not "what." All of humanity is looking for someone. Men and women want their Creator, and they especially need Him when the graves of their lives seem abandoned and desecrated.

Who are you looking for? The remains of your dead Savior? The corpse of your King? Please note with me that who you are looking for could very well determine who you find. Four times, Mary said "Him."

"Where have you taken *Him*?

"If you have taken *Him*...I will go and take Him back.

"I want *Him*. I want the Jesus who cast seven devils out me. I want the Jesus who accepted me when I was trash.

"I'm crying because He's gone, and His absence has left a gaping hole in my heart. I'm looking for Him because if I don't find Him, I might die."

"Jesus said to her 'Mary'." There it is! We just read one of the most powerful statements in the New Testament.

The first words of Jesus Christ after His resurrection from the dead were these: "Mary, why are you crying and who are you looking for?" Oh, thank You, Jesus, for loving humanity. Thank You for trading the royal robes of Heaven for the garb of a gardener (or was that the royal robe of Heaven?).

Thank You for finding Mary. I thought for sure that Peter would be on Your mind. I was just certain You would want to comfort John. What about Your own mother? Weren't You focused on the billions of people who would believe on You as a result of your exploits on the cross? How is it that You were so focused on Mary? How is it that You care about me?

We are so often plagued by the big-picture questions like, "Why do bad things happen to good people?" I'm more perplexed by the question, "How could a God like You remember someone like me?" Why Mary? Why me? Why did You care enough to visit her personally? Oh, visit me!

31

God sees your pain. He hears your cry. He knows why you are crying, but He wants to hear about it from you. He knows who you are looking for. He knows what you have lost. Run to Him. Someday He will make everything right. Revelation 21:4 (NASB) promises that *"He will wipe away every tear from their eyes; and there will no longer be any death; there will no longer be any mourning, or crying, or pain; the first things have passed away."* Mary recognized Him when He called her by name. She didn't recognize Him because of her angelic visitation or because of the folded grave clothes. She recognized Him when she saw that He recognized her. He called her by name. He knew who she was and what was in her heart. He knows the deepest whispers of every heart.

In *The Whisper Test*, Mary Ann Bird writes:

I grew up knowing I was different, and I hated it. I was born with a cleft palate, and when I started school, my classmates made it clear to me how I looked to others: a little girl with a misshapen lip, crooked nose, lopsided teeth, and garbled speech.

When schoolmates asked, "What happened to your lip?" I'd tell them I'd fallen and cut it on a piece of glass. Somehow it seemed more acceptable to have suffered an accident than to have been born different. I was convinced that no one outside my family could love me.

There was, however, a teacher in the second grade whom we all adored—Mrs. Leanord. She was short, round, happy—a sparkling lady.

Annually we had a hearing test...Mrs. Leonard gave the test to everyone in the class, and finally it was my turn. I knew from past years that as we stood against the door and covered one ear, the teacher sitting at her desk would whisper something, and we would have to repeat it back—things like "The sky is blue" or "Do you have new shoes?" I waited there for those words that God must have put into her mouth, those seven words that changed my life. Mrs. Leonard said, in her whisper, "I wish you were my little girl."[5]

You are His daughter. You are His son.

Did you finish the text? Did you notice that Mary stopped crying? Believe it or not, some day so will you!

3

Adam's Triumph

So did I fail? Did you? The question can haunt us. Today, I'm truly convinced that I did my part in pursuing Alexis' miracle. To the best of my ability, I stood after having done all to stand. I do believe the Lord was pleased with my pursuit, and yet she wasn't healed. I know she's whole now in Heaven, but that wasn't my idea of recovering all. What happened?

Should I have prayed a little harder? Should I have had more faith? Did I harbor any doubt in my soul? The answer to all three of these questions is yes. Of course I could have prayed harder. Sure, I could have quoted one more Scripture. My faith probably did waver when I personally changed the trach in her little throat, but that's not the issue.

We can always do *more*. What plagued me was did I do *enough*?

In all honesty, faith was never an issue for me. I studied every reference in the Bible to divine healing. I researched the Hebrew and Greek origins of the words, and I spent at least an hour each day (some days far longer) in true, biblical meditation where I spoke the Word over her little body. Jessica and I played cassette tapes containing healing Scriptures set to music in her room at night while the nurses watched her. We took her to healing services all over the state of Washington and even Canada. I was convinced that the Lord was about to heal her. I even told the doctors that someday she would personally thank them for caring for her with such dignity and tenderness. I had faith.

I never dreamed we would lose her. Even near the end of her life when, due to the tremendous suffering she was experiencing, I was praying, "Lord, either heal her or take her home," I still knew He *could* heal her, and I was still very confident that He *would.* Unbelief was not our downfall. Our church had enough agreement. We had fasted and prayed and bound and loosed and commanded and interceded more than was necessary for a miracle. We didn't fail, and yet on August 26, 1999, she died and ascended to Heaven where she runs and worships and waits for us now.

I don't believe that death is the ultimate failure, but to the living it sure feels like it is. Alexis is with Jesus! That *can't* be failure; however, I'm now battling to rebuild my faith, and for a long time, I *felt* like a failure. Many divorced people feel that way after the final papers are signed. So do some of the unemployed.

So did father Adam. Thank God, the Lord spoke to him and, in doing so, set a precedent for you and me.

"Adam, don't you understand that I always hide victory inside defeat?"

Although I can't prove it to you with a specific Scripture, I'm convinced that God spoke these words to Adam in the midst of his heartbreak outside the Garden of Eden. Adam needed to hear these words. So did I. You probably do too.

In the minds of many, there is truly no greater failure in Scripture than Adam. Some would say that if you or I looked up the word *failure* in a Webster's dictionary, we would see for a definition a picture of Adam standing outside the Garden of Eden. It's true that Adam missed God's will more profoundly than any other person who has ever lived did. It's also true that this missing of God's will—this sin—had greater repercussions than any other sin.

Other failures pale beside his blunder. His error was far worse than Samson's was. It was worse than Judas Iscariot's betrayal of Jesus. Indeed, it was even worse than his son Cain's murder of Abel. You see, Cain killed Abel, but Adam killed mankind. You can thank Adam for your wrinkles and gray hair. You can thank him for the sin nature you were wrestling with this weekend. People might be correct in thinking that Adam ranks right up there with lucifer for the scope of his stupidity and failure.

Please, before you toss this book aside in indignation against this criticism of father Adam, note with me that the study and understanding of the initial chapters of Genesis are incredibly important for our understanding of mankind. We cannot overdo a study of Genesis and the account of the creation of man. Each detail of the story of Adam and Eve is rich with insight that reveals profound truth about humanity. Studying the Book of Genesis (beginning/origins) can help us understand why we are the way we are. It can reveal why we possess some of our basic weaknesses and propensities to certain affections and desires and sorrows.

If you would spend a moment with me examining father Adam and mother Eve, we could glean valuable insight into the grief of mankind as well as a strategy for how to overcome it.

No one failed more dismally and more completely than father Adam did, and consequently, no one grieved more deeply than he.

Think of what he lost! He had God all to himself! Adam experienced what no other human has, or will ever, experience. Today, we tell the saints, "God loves you like you were the only one on the planet." For Adam, that was true! Literally! Before he lost a rib and gained a wife, he experienced a season of life where he was the sole, undistracted focus of all the love and affection of Heaven. The mission statement of Heaven in one word is "family." Adam was it, and he threw the relationship away.

Adam also betrayed his wife. He was present when the serpent tempted Eve. The Scripture tells us that Eve was deceived by the serpent while Adam was not. He wasn't deceived because, prior to this tragic interchange, he had been given the task of naming the animals. The command from God to name the animals was a command for Adam to assert his sovereignty over them. Naming a thing implies the assignment of value, and as he stared into the eyes of every creeping and crawling animal, he knew their nature and value. He knew what was in the serpent—he had named it a snake—and still, he allowed it to molest his wife.

He betrayed her through his silence, and now, men in the 21st century struggle to find their voice. We struggle to speak up for God. We struggle to talk to our wives and to tell our teenage daughters that they are gorgeous royalty fit for a palace. We struggle to tell them that they are fine china rather than a plastic dish or Tupperware. We're trying to regain our voice.

Thanks, Adam!

Sadly, his betrayal of Eve cost him more than his voice. His betrayal released a curse on Eve so she could never again produce life apart from pain, sorrow, and suffering. Dear ladies, please realize you are still bearing the grief of Eve. This betrayal-induced curse not only hurt Eve, but it banned their children forever from Paradise. For Cain and Seth and their offspring, the Garden of Eden would be nothing more than a story—a stinging reminder of daddy's failure.

Can you imagine the heartache? "I've experienced a paradise that my children will never know."

Imagine the grief! "I've walked with God in the garden at the cool of the day, and now Cain, Abel, and Seth will have to dig up thistles and plow hard, thorny ground."

What loss! "I can't even tell them about Eden because if I do, they won't understand. They'll either get angry with God or reject me as their father.

"I noticed the hair around Eve's temples is turning gray— it's my fault!

"People have been dying of disease. There would be no disease had I not sinned.

"I'm standing over Abel's grave, and Cain has just fled from the presence of the Lord—and it's all my fault!" Oh, the screams of anguish he must have shrieked in the wilderness.

Talk about tension in a marriage! It's very possible that Cain and Abel were twins. In the text that records their birth, there is reference to only one conception but two births. Eve's first delivery—her first attempt to produce life—contained double the pain. Yes, of course the joy of a new baby eclipses the pain of labor; but one day Cain would kill Abel, and we just know that she had to ask the question, "Adam, why? I know I was wrong too, but why didn't you protect me in Eden?"

Today, we have a generation that marry and divorce according to the nature of the first Adam within them. Men grieve the loss of their voice—"I can't make her happy. I feel like a failure." Women grieve their isolation—"He doesn't really love me. I can't count on him."

The question hangs in the air through the centuries: "Adam, why?"

ॐ

Sometimes, in moments of extreme isolation and frustration and despair, Adam snuck back to Eden. Oh, I can't prove it to you biblically, but I'm certain that he did. When the Lord drove them out of Eden, He didn't drive them halfway around the world. Adam knew where Eden was. How could he ever forget? He cried a trail of tears in the dust as he left Paradise behind him.

Let's do a little spying. Let's hide together behind some boulders just outside Eden and check on our father—the father of mankind.

It's nearly evening. The day's work is complete. Tomorrow will be the same. Labor, sweat, toil. Thistles, thorns, and weeds. Oh, Adam! How far you have fallen from those glorious moments in the cool of the day with your Creator. I imagine the evenings are the worst. Evening was your special time with the Lord, wasn't it? The cool of the day must freeze your heart outside of Eden. Memories of the loss must drive you nearly mad.

Do you hear that? Someone is coming. They're trying to be stealthy, but they can scarcely contain their weeping. They are approaching very silently—trying to avoid detection. In fact, if not for the muffled sobs, I probably wouldn't have heard them at all. Get down! Here they come.

Wait a second—it's Adam! Do you see him? What is he doing so close to Eden? Why would he risk death at the hands of the cherubim? Oh, Adam…

I can hear him cry. He's hiding from the cherubim, hunkered down, and sobbing in the dirt: "I really am the dirt that He created me from. I should have dominion over those angels—instead if I get too close, they'll take my head off."

Laying in the dirt, wracked in grief and despair, Adam imparts to mankind—to you and me—an unquenchable desire to return to Paradise and an extreme despair that says we never will. Can you hear him?

"I must get back to Paradise. I was made for something more. Oh, but my failure! My loss! I'll never return. The joy I sense should be mine will elude me forever. I have failed, and my failure is final.

"My failure is so final that several thousand years from now, the precious followers of Jesus will be wrestling with a sin nature that I imparted.

"My failure is so final that Jesus will have to come as the 'last Adam' to undo what I, the 'first Adam,' have done."

৵

Truly there is no greater failure in Scripture than Adam. Yet, since his failure eclipses any other failure in Scripture, his grief also eclipses any other grief in Scripture. Adam endured the greatest grief in Scripture. No one failed more dismally than Adam did, and no one suffered more deeply than Adam did. Not even Job.

Job is typically our pinnacle picture of suffering. He lost his children, his fortune, and his health; and when seeking comfort from his friends, he found rebuke. Job's trial was indeed devastating, and it pales many subsequent cases of suffering. Despite the severity of Job's loss, however, scholars tell us that his entire ordeal lasted only about nine months before the Lord restored his fortune. Please hear me: In giving Job's grief a lesser position than Adam's I am not in any way diminishing the deep sorrow of Job.

Although Job's fortune was restored in nine months, he never forgot his first seven children. I doubt the wound ever fully healed on this side of eternity. I would like to point out though, that while the Lord doubled all the land, herds, flocks, and wealth that Job had lost, He didn't double the number of Job's children. He *didn't* give him 14 new sons and daughters. The reason for this displays some of the sweetness of the Lord and can be of great comfort for those who have lost loved ones. When the Lord set out to double all that Job had lost, He didn't consider his children to be lost. *They were with Him!* Job would be joined with them for eternity! The pain of their absence was devastatingly real, but the veil separating the family was very thin; and in the Lord's eyes, they weren't really gone. Giving Job seven new children *did* double his children! The Lord also gave him 140 years in peace to watch his grandchildren grow up before his eyes.

Job's devastation was epic in proportion, but nothing like Adam's. The Lord restored the fortune of Job, but if Adam ever attempted to set foot in the garden again, the cherubim would have impaled him on their fiery swords. Job lived 140 years in restoration, watching his grandchildren on his knees. Adam lived over eight hundred years outside the Garden of Eden watching the fruit of his sin unfold.

Oh, Adam!

Do you know what I respect the most about Adam? He never committed suicide! Suicide would have been easier for him than living eight centuries in grief. For eight hundred years, humanity hungered and suffered and wept and slowly forgot the seed of paradise in their hearts—thanks to Adam.

Having painted this grim picture, let me now build a case that will show that Adam (the greatest failure of humanity) became the greatest overcomer in Scripture. Yes, we've tasted of Adam's failure—we live with it every day. We feel it on birthdays. We see it in the mirror as age takes its toll on our physical bodies. Despite his failure, however, there was enough of the image of God left in him to allow him to somehow rekindle a fresh fire in the ashes of his burned-out life. Yes, you and I have tasted of Adam's failure, but today, we can also taste of Adam's triumph!

༄

Lying in the bushes, hiding from the angels, tears forming mud in the dirt around his face, Adam hears the Lord begin to speak. "My son, let's review.

"Your failure was not great enough to derail My plan for mankind.

"In fact, before I laid the foundation of the world, Jesus and I talked about you, and We made a little plan. Before the serpent ever slithered into the garden, Jesus told Me that in the event that you were injured and fell, He would come to earth and sort things out.

"Adam, listen to Me! He isn't called the 'last Adam' as an indictment *against* you. He's called the 'last Adam' because He wants to identify *with* you.

"Adam, hear Me! I want you to understand something. *I always hide victory inside defeat.*

"You thought you were being cursed when I said the serpent would bruise your heel? I was trying to tell you that even in defeat, you would crush his head!

"You thought I was punishing you by asking you to till the ground and pull up thorns? I was actually making you a picture of the last Adam who will come to rip the curse off the earth.

"Oh, you thought I was angry when I said you had eaten fruit of the knowledge of good and evil, and therefore, you couldn't eat from the tree of life? Please try to understand Me, Adam. When I named the first tree the 'knowledge of good and evil,' I chose a very strategic word for knowledge. I chose a word that will come to mean experiential or sexual knowledge. It's the type of *knowledge* that means to become one with something. The word I used for evil means an inability to measure up to My good standards that will benefit. When you and Eve ate that particular fruit, all of Heaven gasped. Angels rushed to My side crying, 'Lord, they have just become one with an inability to measure up to Your plan and Your best standards!' Adam, on the heels of such tragedy, I would never have allowed you and Eve to eat from the tree of life and live forever in that state. I refuse to allow you to live forever with an inability to measure up to My plan for you. In fact, I'd rather let you die...and then resurrect you into a better Eden where we will walk together for eternity!

"You thought the cherubim were keeping you away from Paradise? Actually, they're keeping you away from your place of failure. Adam, even if you could sneak past them, you wouldn't find paradise. Eden is dying with you. The game plan has changed. No, I'm sorry, but no one from Earth will ever find Eden. No one will ever again be born there. But, Adam, if you are still willing to walk with Me in the cool of the day, if you are still willing to do your part, mankind can return again to Eden. And, Adam, the end result will be even better than what you lost.

"Your failure certainly did not quench My desire for family. More than ever I desire to walk in the cool of the day with My sons and daughters. If they'll walk with Me, I can refresh them from some of the toil they have been forced to live.

"Think about this with Me. I spent only six days creating this paradise that you so loved. When Jesus comes to earth, He will tell His questioning disciples that when He leaves their planet, He will begin preparing a place for them. First, Adam, if you liked what I made in six days, imagine what He will do in over 2,000 years! My precious son, your failure certainly cannot eclipse that!"

ॐ

When the Lord finished speaking and Adam looked up, I think he saw the cherubim in a different light. The very gate that blocked Paradise had become a gateway of hope.

"I thought he set up a gate to keep me *out*—in reality He painted a picture of how I could get back *in*.

"*I* am to be a cherub with a flaming sword that turns every way. No one will ever experience the fire of the presence of God as I experienced it in the Garden of Eden. I have a responsibility. I must devote the remainder of my life—even if it is eight hundred more years—to being a guardian and a keeper of that flame."

Then the spirit of the last Adam entered into the soul of the first Adam and he arose, wiping tear-stained cheeks, and became the greatest keeper of the world's greatest flame. I wager that the cherubim saluted him. I bet in that moment, he looked like the image of God again!

Please let me remind you that while he may have been the first Adam, he was not the first keeper of the flame. Isaiah 42:3

(NASB) says "*...a dimly burning wick He* [the last Adam] *will not extinguish.*" As God Himself crouched in the bushes with Adam, He said to him, "I am the flame, and I am the keeper of the flame; and you are still made in My image. Son, I'll never quench your fire, and I'll always empower you to guard the fire in others."

Now perhaps it is more understandable why Moses saw a burning bush in the desert. Maybe God saw Moses as a discouraged son of Adam with his flame about to go out. Perhaps He remembered the day when He and Adam looked between the branches of a bush into the flaming sword of the keepers of the flame. I wonder if He thought, *I'm going to paint a picture here— just for Adam and Me!*

Filled with fresh fire and resolve, Adam arose with the thought, "I'm going to try again. I'm going to know my wife again. I'm going to pass the fire on to another son, and this son will be named Seth which means 'appointed.'

"Amidst my disappointment, the Lord has scheduled another appointment for me. He has created another opportunity to ignite a flame in a generation. And by the time Seth is a father, an entire generation will be set on fire, and they will begin to call on the name of the Lord!" I'm glad that Adam pressed on in spite of his deep discouragement.

William Wilberforce, who was instrumental in the abolition of slavery in Great Britain, also pressed on despite a deep sense of discouragement and failure. Carol Porter wrote of him in *Leadership Journal*:

> For years William Wilberforce pushed Britain's Parliament to abolish slavery. Discouraged, he was about to give up. His elderly friend, John Wesley, heard of it and from his deathbed called for pen and paper.
>
> With trembling hand, Wesley wrote: "Unless God has raised you up for this very thing, you will be worn out by the opposition of men and devils. But if God be for

you, who can be against you? Are all of them stronger than God?

"Oh be not weary of well-doing! Go on, in the name of God and in the power of His might, till even American slavery shall vanish away before it."

Wesley died six days later, but Wilberforce fought for forty-five more years and in 1833, three days before his own death, saw slavery abolished in Britain.

Even the greatest ones need encouragement.[6]

Please note with me, that Genesis 5:1-5 contains the Scripture that we referenced in the Introduction. It says that Adam "*lived.*" This is our Hebrew word *chayah,* and it means to live again. Adam lived and died in Eden, and then he began to live again!

Noah experienced this life too. One of the most promising verses in Scripture gets lost in the genealogies of Genesis chapter 9. It says in verse 28 that "*After the flood* [and the devastation of his world] *Noah lived* [chayah]" (NIV). Dear one, so will you. In the next chapter, Noah will show us how.

4

You Will Live Again!

Noah's ark. The story has become a symbol of the love and mercy of God. Little children in Sunday school classes know the story, and they even identify the rainbow as the sign of God's covenant with mankind.

My four-year-old daughter, Amber, knows the story. She sings songs about Noah and his floating zoo. It's a sweet story.

Sort of.

While Noah's ark is indeed a story of God's eternal love and His commitment to the destiny of mankind, it is also a story of great devastation. It's a story of death. It's a story of annihilation.

I used to like it until I began to identify too closely with Noah. I know God loves me, and I know that He will someday work all this out for good. I believe Him when He says I didn't fail, so why does my world look so flat? Why can't I even recognize the sky?

C.S. Lewis said after the loss of his wife to cancer, "The act of living is different all through. Her absence is like the sky, spread over everything."[7] I can relate to that. Sometimes I'm not even sure I'm me.

I used to read Noah's ark as a story of God's redemption of mankind until I found myself surrounded by death.

It really is quite a story.

There has never been, nor will there ever again be, an event that causes as much devastation as Noah's great flood. It broke the foundations of the earth, restructured the face of the planet, and killed every human being except for Noah and his immediate family. It even changed the color of the sky.

I'm not trying to paint a grim perspective on the most beloved of Sunday school stories. My desire is to reveal a glimpse of the amazing, overcoming mercy of God that was eventually displayed through Noah's agonizing experience.

We see this mercy in Genesis 9 when the Holy Spirit says, *"After the flood Noah lived"* (NIV). We've seen that the word *lived* means to live again, but it also means to recover and to enjoy life. Noah faced the literal crushing of his world, and then he began to live again. How did he do it? How do we? Let's peek inside this sweet Sunday school story and let Noah teach us.

꒳

Poor Noah! The swimming inside his head reflected the swirling chaos of water, wind, and destruction that was raging outside the ark. Seasick for the first time in his six hundred years of life, he sprawled in a corner beside a rather angry-looking rhinoceros, helpless to do anything but vomit. He had no idea where his wife was on this floating zoo, and quite frankly, he didn't care.

Thirty-nine days and thirty-nine nights ago they had stood holding hands in awe of the magnificent display of God's glory as every imaginable beast streamed into the ark. The procession was staggering in its beauty. Lions beside lambs and zebras beside armadillos, the array of mammals and reptiles and creeping things defied description. The sky above the animals darkened as thousands of birds and flying creatures swept down upon the scene. Plumage of every imaginable color shimmered in the fading sunlight, and the screams and caws and whistles and roars and neighs were almost deafening. Hand in hand, Noah and the wife of his youth watched the tableau with a mixture of fear and wonder and worship. Arm in arm, they slowly entered the ark behind the last pair of turtles and sloths. Cuddling tight, they gasped as the Lord Himself closed the door of the ark. Embracing for comfort and security, they listened to the thunder blasts that rent the heavens and released the greatest deluge of water and violence the earth would ever endure. Thirty-nine days earlier he had clung to his sweet wife and shared whispered prayers of gratitude. Tonight, he clung to the rump of an angry rhino, wishing he could banish his sense of smell forever.

☞

When Noah received the mandate from the Lord to build the ark, he had no idea what the implications would be. He had no idea that he would endure a century of trial, ridicule, and loneliness, and that the *end* of that century would mark the *beginning* of the real disorientation and loss. He had no idea that he and his family would witness the most brutal devastation of mankind in the history of the world. There was no way for him to imagine the extreme pain they would suffer.

When God commissioned Noah, he was five hundred years old. He loved his family. He loved His God. He wept over the evil and perversion that permeated the earth. While the stories of Adam and Eve in the Garden of Eden had all but vanished from the hearts of mankind, they burned with increasing intensity in his own breast. He cried for days after his visitation and commissioning from the Lord. He sensed he had been born for such an hour.

Even convincing his wife of the calling had been easy. She was a woman of faith. She had to be. Married for hundreds of years to a fanatical believer like Noah had pulled the saint out of her, and she responded to the word of the Lord with incredible reverence and faith.

The centuries he spent in faithfulness, sacrifice, and endurance were merely the preparations for this moment in time. His family had been chosen to propagate the holy seed of God. They would save humanity!

The first few months of the venture proved inspiring and rewarding. Despite the skepticism and sarcasm from neighbors and superficial friends, Noah felt the presence and purpose of God. He made his preparations and went about his task like a knight on a kingly errand. The criticism fueled his resolve. The absurdity of the vision verified that it must be divine. He worked and worshipped and didn't pay the slightest heed to opposition.

That was the first few months.

Ninety-nine years and eleven months later the grace had waned substantially. He had spent his fortune on gopher wood and pitch and survival rations and food for a king-sized zoo. His friends had long since ceased to be amused, and they no longer even commented on the fact that water never fell from Heaven. Landlocked, broke, and desperately hoping that his encounter with God hadn't been a midlife crisis hallucination, Noah put the finishing touches on the ark and admired his handiwork.

Square and sticky with pitch and slime, the ark was a monstrosity. Row after row of animal stalls filled its dark interior, and the pleased look in Noah's eyes as he viewed it only confirmed his insanity. His poor wife had endured the process with fidelity and devotion (although there is never *any* indication in Scripture that the Lord ever spoke to her directly about the flood). She had said good-bye to countless friends and lovingly thanked her sons and daughters-in-law for dutifully helping their father for the better part of a century. What a woman! What a man!

It had been a century-long bout with questions and confusion. It had been a century-long fight of faith and doubt and belief and anxiety. They had faced a hundred years of ridicule and scorn. They had become regular characters in the cartoon section of the local newspaper. Without a single drop of rain, there had been no confirmation to his initial encounter with God. *Before* the near extinction of mankind, Noah and his family were alone. It was a century-long dark night of the soul.

And then the flood came.

For a few brief moments at the beginning of the flood, there was a sense of elation and awe. Very quickly, however, the realization dawned that humanity would not be spared. As the screams of mankind mingled with the screams of thunder and storm clouds, the reality crashed home. They were alone.

When the flood abated, it was only Noah and his seven family members on their floating zoo. You and I in the 21st century can't even fathom the loneliness.

What about the bodies? They didn't all disappear in the flood. They were everywhere! Animal stench and death surrounded them.

After the forty days and nights of raging storms had ended, and they waited another several months on the ark, they were finally able to exit their floating zoo and behold the new world. One of the first things they noticed was that the very topography of their world had changed.

Many scientists believe that prior to the flood, there was only one continent with no inland seas. They believe that the fury of the great flood broke up the earth's surface and separated the landmass into the arrangement of our modern-day continents. How shocking it must have been for Noah and his family to view this rearrangement of their world.

This was no superficial, cosmetic change of scenery. The very foundational landmasses of their world had changed. They didn't have a skewed perspective due to their trauma—their world was different, and it would never be the same. If the water had suddenly evaporated, they would have still been unable to find their way home. They no longer had a home.

It wasn't just the scenery. The very color of their world had changed. Some scientists also believe that the pre-flood sky was not blue. Do you remember the vapor canopy that the Lord used to water the earth? Instead of precipitation in the form of rainfall, the Lord caused a mist to arise from the ground to water the earth. This mist would have refracted the sunlight as it touched the planet's water canopy and created a prism effect.

It is quite likely that the pre-flood sky was a myriad of rainbow colors. When Noah lifted his eyes to Heaven, he didn't gaze into a sea-blue sky; he beheld a brilliant array of the entire color scheme. Perhaps this was the significance of the rainbow that the Lord used to mark His covenant with Noah. The rainbow was a reminder of life before destruction.

Try to imagine the sick, sinking feeling Noah's family must have experienced as they opened the ark and beheld a flat, gray sky. The color had literally drained out of their world. Their vision was dulled.

I can say from brutal experience that in times of deep loss a gray pallor seems to hang over the sky. It doesn't matter how blistering the sun may actually be. Everything feels cold. C.S. Lewis said it another way. After the death of his wife, Joy, he said, "The world is like a mean street."[8]

It's here in the annals of Genesis that our profound, little verse is found. Genesis 9:28, says *"After the flood Noah lived."* After what? After the devastation of his world, a century-long trial, ridicule, abandonment, loneliness, fear, a terrible change in scenery, the loss of color and vision, and the surrounding presence of death, Noah lived. After all this, he lived!

I have five promises from the Lord for you regarding your loss and the devastation of your world.

Promise #1: There is an after.

Genesis 9:28 says, *"After* the flood." This gruesome ordeal was only 1/9 of Noah's life. Yes, he spent a century building the ark, but he lived to be 950 years old. He did live again. The earth was repopulated. He planted a vineyard (I think he deserved a little wine, don't you?). God still formed a chosen people through Noah's seed. Jesus still came to earth, died, stripped the keys from satan, rose from the dead, and ascended to Heaven so He could give us the Holy Spirit so we could change the world. There *is* an after. He lived *again*! Noah's destiny was not to build an ark and endure a worldwide destruction. His destiny was to raise up godly sons and daughters who would replenish and rule the earth. The Lord's dealings, adjustments, and restructuring of his life were all bringing him closer to his "after." Yours too!

Promise #2: You will live *again*.

You will live again. You will love again. Your destiny is not over. Your passion and zest for life will return. Your only job is to keep living and stay tender before the Lord even while you wrestle with your loose ends. He will raise you to life again. You are not destined to grieve for eternity!

Promise #3: You will enjoy life again.

You'll recover your joy. Believe it or not, jokes will be funny again. Smiles won't always be fake. C.S. Lewis went on to say of his dear wife's memory, "I will turn to her as often as possible in gladness. I will even salute her with a laugh."[9] The ability to laugh and love and enjoy aspects of life again does not detract from the severity of the loss. You are not destined for a hollow life of pain-wracked grief. You will smile again.

Promise #4: You will see.

Our verse says that you will live again. This same phrase was used of Joseph and Job; however, with these men, the Holy Spirit added a few words. Genesis 50:22-23 says, "*And Joseph lived one hundred and ten years. Joseph saw Ephraim's children to the third generation*" (emphasis added). Job 42:16 says, "*After this* [after death, bankruptcy, sickness, and heartache] *Job lived one hundred and forty years,* **and saw** *his children and grandchildren for four generations"* (emphasis added).

You will see. Your sight will be restored. You'll receive vision again. I should warn you, however, that you will see differently. Your world has changed, and it will never look the same. You won't see people the same way. You won't see God the same way.

What did Joseph and Job see? They saw the generations. They saw the hope that was following them, even after trial and trauma and tragedy. If we allow God to have His work in us, He will use crisis to elevate us above our present moment into a bigger perspective. We are merely a part of God's plan for the ages.

Promise #5: Not only will you continue to live, but you will also *recover all the passion and zeal that you have lost.*

If you *re-*cover, it means you were *un-*covered, thus vulnerable and exposed. I'm still trying to re-cover some areas of my life—especially my passion and zeal.

My passion and zeal have been the slowest things to return to me as I've recovered. I haven't lost my love for the Lord, just a portion of my zeal. I still love Him as much as ever—possibly more. I love His presence and I love His Word, but disappointment has taken some of the passion out of my soul. It's a by-product of grief. Passions wane in the hurting heart, and the desire to fight is snuffed out.

I heard that D.L. Moody was asked in the twilight of his life how he continued to preach and carry on under the weight of ministry. His reply was as sweet as it was profound. He said, "I never lost the wonder." I've lost it many times. How do I get it back? Life on its own will not sustain the wonder. Life will eventually turn gray (even for the Christian), and the problem with the wonder and the zeal of the Lord is that they are very easy to lose. In fact, they're the first things to go during flood season.

Here's how it works. We meet God, and our hearts are enflamed. We join the fellowship of the burning heart, and our passionate zeal compels us to pay the price. We take the time and the effort to build a strong relationship with the Lord through the disciplines of prayer, fasting, Bible meditation, and fellowship. We greet the dawn in our anticipation of a few more minutes in His presence. We are regular fixtures at every church function. We fall in love with Him deeply and truly. It's wonderful—until flood season hits.

When floods threaten to restructure our world, the first thing to leave is our zeal. We still love Him. We're still in relationship with Him. We haven't lost our salvation—only our wonder. The firm foundation of relationship holds us during the storm, and we survive. But when we emerge from our personal ark, things are different. We love Him, and we're committed to Him; but the sky looks flat and gray. We've lost our wonder. That's okay!

It's okay if you realize that you've begun to approach Him at arm's length. You know how we do it. We pray, give our tithes, and participate in worship; but our life isn't wrapped around His Word like it used to be. We live like the believer in Acts who said they hadn't even heard if there was a Holy Spirit (see Acts 19:2). It's okay to get to this point, but He doesn't want us to stay there. The Lord wants us to recover all the life we have lost. He wants to restore our wonder.

Psalm 28:8-9 says He carries His anointed. Let Him carry you. If grief makes you lose your place in your daily Bible reading schedule, pick it up again next month. He loves you. He desires you!

The Lord won't leave you in the valley forever. He is just, and He is seasonal. It would be unjust to leave a blanket of icy, winter cold over the face of the earth for too long. He's too just, and He loves you too much. The wonder will return and you will live again!

After the flood, Noah lived. So did Job. So did Joseph. All that the Lord required of them was to lie in His arms and hold on tight. When they were thus positioned, the reviving power of the Lord settled over them, and today, they are testimonies that what was meant for evil, *"God meant it for good...to save many people alive"* (Gen. 50:20).

There is a tender verse in the Song of Solomon where the friends of the bride and bridegroom ask, *"Who is this coming up from the wilderness, leaning upon her beloved?"* (Song 8:5) What had happened to her? They recognized her before her wilderness experience, but she had changed in the desert. I know it was a positive thing that she was leaning more closely on the lover of her soul, but the fact remains that she was different. I, too, am very different after my days in the wilderness. Yes, God has dealt with my flesh, and that is important; but I think I've lost some of me in the process. My personality has been altered. I have far more compassion for humanity, but I'm also far more fragile. I must lean or I can't stand. I'm so grateful that He's promised my recovery.

I'm grateful that Noah lived and recovered and laughed and saw. He went through enough devastation in his day. I'm glad he's basking in the warm glow of Heaven today, and I'm glad he set a precedent for me. I'm glad the Scriptures say that I, too, can live again.

Psalm 71:20 says, *"You, who have shown me great and severe troubles, shall revive me again."* The word *revive* is the Hebrew word *nacham*, and it means to draw the breath forcibly. It's a type of mouth-to-mouth resuscitation. The patient in need of this reviving can only lie on the floor and wait for the breath to be forced back into their lungs. I'm not sure if I can scale a tall mountain right now, but I know I can lie in His presence and wait for His reviving power.

So can you.

Let's commit right now that it will be said of us, "After their flood and the devastation of their worlds, they lived. They lived again! Their joy returned! They loved God even more! If they lived, then so can I."

5

The Biblical Response to Grief

I pursued as a man of God. How do I grieve as one? I tried to please Him in my fight of faith. How do I please Him now that that particular battle is over? Oh, I'm not done fighting. Now I'm fighting for my soul. I'm fighting for my faith and my perspective of the goodness of God. I still love Him, but life doesn't make sense.

Does the Bible teach us how to grieve? I know it teaches us how to worship and how to pray for the impossible. I know it reveals the heart of God for humanity. But is there a blueprint that can help us navigate the minefields of heartache, loss, and grief? I believe there is.

There is a powerful principle in Bible study called the law of first mention. This principle simply states that the first mention of a word or theme or concept in Scripture is very significant in defining it. The details of the first mention of a thing help define the thing. For example, the first mention of the word *prophet* is in the context of the Lord speaking to Abimelech about Sarah, Abraham's wife. The Lord says to Abimelech, "[Abraham] *is a prophet, and he will pray for you*" (Gen. 20:7). Applying the law of first mention for a prophet, then, we learn that a prophet's primary responsibility is not prophecy, but prayer. This makes perfect sense because the fresh, anointed, prophetic word only comes from the presence of the Lord. Well, what is the law of first mention regarding *grief*? Biblically, how should I grieve? Is there a model that I can follow? I don't want to grieve as *"others who have no hope"* (1 Thess. 4:13), and yet I'm dying. I don't want to stuff my grief and end up with health problems later in life. How does a man of God grieve? How does a woman of faith endure loss and trauma?

The law of first mention in Scripture regarding grief comes after the death of Sarah, the faithful wife of Abraham and mother of Isaac. The Scripture gives us insights into the response of both husband and son that are deeply liberating. Indeed they set us up for a healthy, thorough, balanced approach to grief, faith, and healing.

I begin this study of Abraham and Isaac's heartache with a fair amount of trepidation. I'm a little anxious as I attempt to share these insights, because I know the extreme vulnerability of sorrow and grief. Those who are experiencing the deep pain of loss are very sensitive, and it is easy to unwittingly inflict guilt or condemnation on them. Let me say up front that when the Bible addresses the subject of grief, it offers principles rather than formulas. If your experience is slightly different from what is presented here with Abraham and Isaac, or if your time frames of mourning vary, please be at peace. It's okay. The principles revealed through Abraham and Isaac's response to loss should be very comforting and encouraging.

Let's begin with Abraham. Our story of Abraham's grief begins in Genesis 23. The beginning of this chapter tells us that Sarah was 127 years old when she passed away. Please keep the following figures in mind as we commence because they will become helpful in assessing the biblical time frames for mourning and grief recovery. Abraham (ten years older than Sarah) was 137 years old, and Isaac was 37 years old at the time of her death.

Genesis 23:2 says, *"Sarah died in Kirjath Arba."* *Kirjath* means "city of," and *Arba* was the name of the chief of the giants who dominated the land at that time. Kirjath Arba was the stronghold of the giants. Abraham and Sarah were in an enemy land when she died. Sometimes grief strikes when the enemy has you surrounded. In a stronghold of the enemy, Abraham lost his wife and was plunged into the icy grasp of grief.

Grief can follow an expected loss such as the death of aged grandparents, but it can also shock you with its unexpected timing. Abraham didn't expect to lose Sarah. He was ten years older than she was. Today, the life expectancy for the average female is several years longer than that of the average man. Abraham should have died first.

"Sarah died in Kirjath Arba (that is, Hebron)." If Kirjath Arba is an unfamiliar term, it's more likely that you've heard of Hebron. Hebron was the mountain that Caleb conquered as an 80-year-old man. It was the mountain where David was first anointed king of Judah. We're scarcely into the study of grief, and the Holy Spirit wants to insert hope. You see, the word Hebron means the seat of association, fellowship, or friendship. Unexpectedly, amidst enemy giants, Sarah died in Kirjath Arba, and yet, the same was Hebron. Abraham needed to understand that the Lord provides a seat in the midst of enemy strongholds. This seat is not a seat of despair, and it is not a seat of defeat. It is a seat of fellowship and association. Oh, how we need the Lord to associate with us in our grief. Thank God that Kirjath Arba was also Hebron!

In *Deliver Us From Evil*, Ravi Zacharias powerfully illustrates this idea of identification. He tells the story of Joseph Damien, a 19th-century missionary who ministered to the leprous individuals who lived on the island of Molokai, Hawaii.

One morning before Damien was to lead daily worship, he was pouring some hot water into a cup when the water swirled out and fell onto his bare foot. It took him a moment to realize that he had not felt any sensation. Gripped by the sudden fear of what this could mean, he poured more hot water on the same spot. No feeling whatsoever.

Damien immediately knew what had happened. As he walked tearfully to deliver his sermon, no one at first noticed the difference in his opening line. He normally began every sermon with, "My fellow believers." But this morning he began with, "My fellow lepers."

In a greater measure Jesus came into this world knowing what it would cost Him. He bore in His pure being the marks of evil, that we might be made pure.[10]

I wonder if Abraham knew that Kirjath Arba was also Hebron. I'm not naive. The fact that the Psalms tell us that the Lord is a "very present help in trouble" doesn't mean our loss or pain is easy. Darkness isn't darkness unless it's dark, and the initial stages of grief can be like midnight. I'm glad the Psalms state that "He dwells in thick darkness" because sometimes we can't see Him in our grief. We reason, "If He were present, this would not have happened." Whether Abraham felt God's presence or not, whether he was seated with God or with enemy giants, we know that he did something very wise. He stayed put.

This is very conventional, but very sound advice: Times of grief are not times for drastic decisions. When giants overrun your seat of security and the routine of your life is shattered by loss, don't move. It is not the time to change churches or careers or faiths. Abraham's initial response to Sarah's death is the first step to responding to loss biblically. He stayed put, and he grieved.

"...and Abraham came to mourn for Sarah and to weep for her." He grieved! He wept! He cried like a baby!

When Abraham left his native country and was first introduced in Scripture, he was 75 years old. Assuming he and Sarah were newlyweds at the time (which is not likely) and applying the math, we know that at a minimum, they were married for 62 years. They were sweethearts. They had lived a long life together. They endured famines together. They faced brutal tests of faith together (some of which they passed and some they failed). They experienced name changes together. Their dreams were fulfilled together. The Lord visited them and restored laughter to their lives. Abraham loved Sarah, and he took time to grieve for her.

There is a time for grief. It is critical that we do the right things in the right seasons. There can be no denial in a time of grief. Grieve! It's dangerous not to grieve after loss. Yes, the Lord does bring grief to an end, and He does dry tears; but He doesn't say, "Since you're a Christian, you must be strong. Don't cry." No! He says in Revelation 21:4 that He will wipe away all tears, but there is *never* rebuke for the shed tears. Abraham came to weep for her.

In the initial stages of loss, we can enter a numb state of shock that, surprisingly, contains very little emotion. Don't mistake this for faith. Some Christians enter this state of shock, and they assume that their lack of emotion is some form of faith or trust. Oh, please hear me. The Lord can and does give strength, and there is a peace and a hope for His children; but it is also appropriate to grieve. Don't worry if you can't stop crying, and don't worry if tears won't flow early on. Don't panic and fear that you're either a basket case or that you are stuffing your emotions; just follow father Abraham's lead. Stay put and take time to mourn.

In this early phase of grief, it is very easy to despair. May I offer a few suggestions to help guide you through this stage.

1. **Trust your relationship with God.** You will probably think irrational thoughts. Since everything is so bleak, you may wonder if God has removed His hand from your life. Will you ever live again? I promise you: He isn't going to betray you. If zeal and passion wane (and they will), trust Him to carry you until you can run again.

2. **Keep the size of God in perspective.** He's the beginning and the end. If you judge Him only by the present circumstance, you will despair. The shortest moment of time is this present moment, but in grief the present moment seems to last for an eternity.

3. **Let others pray for you, even if their prayers don't seem to help.** Let someone else bring you to the throne of God. Rely on someone else's faith. Give someone the blessing of bearing your burden in love.

R. Wayne Willis illustrated this truth in *Leadership Journal.* He said:

A student asked anthropologist Margaret Mead for the earliest sign of civilization in a given culture. He expected the answer to be a clay pot or perhaps a fish hook or grinding stone.

Her answer was: "A healed femur."

Mead explained that no mended bones are found where the law of the jungle, survival of the fittest, reigns. A healed femur shows that someone cared. Someone had to do that injured person's hunting and gathering until the leg healed. The evidence of compassion is the first sign of civilization.[11]

4. **Create your strategy for recovery and do it by faith.** You may not want to attend church meetings or social functions (and that's okay), but some things are still necessary for continued health. When a child is very hungry, water doesn't sound very satisfying, but water is essential for life.

5. **Guard against offense.** Hurting moments are vulnerable moments. The hard knocks of life demolish our defenses leaving us raw and exposed. Our skin seems to thin out, and we become much more sensi-

tive to insult or injury. It seems impossible for people to respond to us correctly. We can be hurt if they
don't ask about our welfare, but we can feel they're
too flippant about it if they do.

6. **Don't panic.** There is a frantic, nervous fear that
   accompanies grief. Hold steady.

7. **Stay in the lifeboat.** Your job is not to overcome
   after trauma. Your job is to lie there and breathe.

Abraham stayed in the lifeboat and he grieved.

The next thing that Abraham did was very significant. He
requested a specific burial place for Sarah. It's extremely important that we choose a safe place to bury our pain. We prayed for
Alexis for three-and-a-half years. Where do we bury our loss?
Should I bury her legacy in bitterness? Anger? Despair? Failure?
Heavens no! Abraham knew that it was critical to express his
grief, and he also knew that it was critical to choose the right resting-place for it. He chose "Machpelah and Mamre." *Machpelah*
means "doubling," and *Mamre* means "fatness." He experienced
loss (subtraction) and he chose doubling. Fatness is often cross-
referenced in Scripture as anointing. Somehow he saw a double
anointing in a time of loss.

Abraham must have known that someday ministry would
emerge from his pain. He must have had an Old Testament revelation of the apostle Paul's New Testament exhortation: "*Sorrow*
[not even] *as others who have no hope*" (1 Thess. 4:13). Abraham
had hope that death wasn't the end. He knew that God would
produce good.

Abraham grieved, but he did his grieving in Hebron and
Machpelah. Mourn your loss, but be careful which resting-place
you choose for your loss. This principle had so transformed
Abraham that he passed it on to his descendants. In the succeeding generations, Isaac buried Rebekah at Machpelah, and Jacob
buried Leah there as well.

Let's pass this knowledge on to our children: *Grief contains potential life.*

Leadership Journal relates a story that illustrates this truth:

Farmers in southern Alabama were accustomed to planting one crop every year—cotton. They would plow as much ground as they could and plant their crop. Year after year they lived by cotton.

Then one year the dreaded boll weevil devastated the whole area. So the next year the farmers mortgaged their homes and planted cotton again, hoping for a good harvest. But as the cotton began to grow, the insect came back and destroyed the crop, wiping out most of the farms.

The few who survived those two years of the boll weevil decided to experiment the third year, so they planted something they'd never planted before—peanuts. And peanuts proved so hardy and the market proved so ravenous for that product that the farmers who survived the first two years reaped profits that third year that enabled them to pay off all their debts. They planted peanuts from then on and prospered greatly.

Then you know what those farmers did? They spent some of their new wealth to erect in the town square a monument—to the boll weevil. If it hadn't been for the boll weevil, they never would have discovered peanuts. They learned that even out of disaster there can be great delight.[12]

Another recovery principle illustrated by Abraham's experience is that loss *will* be replaced. In making this statement, I'm not saying that a lost loved one is replaced. I now have my third daughter, Madelyn Joy. Amber and Madelyn are the delights of my life, but they will never replace their sister—and they were never intended to. After Job lost his seven children, the Lord added seven more to him, but his first seven were still gone. I'm sure he never fully recovered from the pain of his loss. The lost person (or dream, or hope) is not replaced; however, the void created by their loss requires special care. This has nothing to do with forgetting, but with a healthy infilling of God and His provision so we can fully heal.

Our sin natures are so ingrained in us that pride can play right into our grief. C.S. Lewis said we want to grieve on the heroic level—like Greek lovers in a tragic play.[13] We don't want to get *over it* because we think our grief proves our love. It's interesting to me that Abraham remarried.

Abraham grieved, but he left his grief in Machpelah; and then he remarried (see Gen. 25:1). Oh, he never forgot Sarah! He never "got over" the wife of his youth; but he healed, and the evidence of his healing was his ability to love again.

Another sign of Abraham's healing was his care for Isaac. It's normal to look inward and focus on the wounds, and God certainly allows a season for introspective, intense grief; however, a sign of health amidst grief is the ability to care *for others.* Abraham demonstrated this health when, amidst his own pain, he thought of Isaac and responded to his need.

Isaac had a very special relationship with Sarah. She named him *Isaac,* which means "laughter." He was the son of the promise, and he removed the mark of barrenness from her life. His conception and birth introduced her to the radical power of an all-loving God. She drove away his older half-brother, Ishmael, so Isaac would never doubt his place as a son. His grief as a son, while certainly different from the grief of a bereaved husband, was severe.

Genesis 24 is primarily the story of Abraham's search for Isaac's wife. At the chapter's end, when Isaac received Rebekah as his wife, he was finally comforted from Sarah's death. The way that he responded until Rebekah became his wife reveals some practical insights into a healthy response to loss.

The first time we see him after her death is in Genesis 24:62. It says "Isaac came from...." Since he was coming from somewhere, it means he had been moving. It's dangerous to lie for too long. After Jessica's c-sections, the doctors insisted that she get up and walk within 12 hours. We *must* lie for a season so we don't reopen unhealed wounds; however, we must be very careful not to lie too long.

Like the deceptive feeling of warmth that settles over a hypothermic man in a snowstorm, lying too long in the initial stage of grief can invite a spiritual hypothermia. Our spiritual life can die right there. This is the reason that the Lord established a 30-day period for the initial response to bereavement.

Deuteronomy 34:8 says, *"The children of Israel wept for Moses...thirty days. So the days of weeping and mourning for Moses ended."* Don't panic! We'll see in a few moments that the Lord allows a great deal of time for recovery and healing. This Scripture does not say that all grieving is absolutely finished in 30 days. It simply says that, while there is an initial season devoted to hard grief, there comes a time to begin moving again.

After the initial 30 days of grieving ended, they broke camp and traveled again. Everything stopped initially. There *is* a time for introspective, hard grieving, but God limits it because He knows if this stage is unchecked, it can destroy our faith, our hope, and our perspective of God. He never expects our healing to be complete in 30 days, but He *does* ask us to move again because it is very easy for grief to become mired in despair, and despair can bring with it the desire to die.

Job wanted to die. So did Jeremiah. So did Elijah and Jonah. They hurt so badly that they despaired of life—and there was no rebuke from the Lord for these very real emotions. There is nothing wrong with a Christian experiencing such pain and grief that he or she desires to die; however, we can't stay in this place. He wants us to live again!

Since Isaac "*came from the way of the well*" (Gen. 24:62 KJV), we see that he must have grieved appropriately. He lay down and then he arose and walked.

Please receive this caution: The victim of hard grief is seldom the right person to analyze his or her own progress. If you are mourning deep loss, it's true that your friends probably don't understand your pain, but you still need their watchful care. Be accountable with your grief. Jessica and I needed different counsel at the different stages of mourning. Some days we needed to be released to grieve. At other times, we needed to try to walk again.

When Isaac began walking again, he didn't walk aimlessly. Genesis 24:62 says he "*came from the way of the well of Lahai Roi*" (KJV). To understand the significance of this particular well, we must quickly review its history.

Hagar, the mother of Isaac's half-brother, Ishmael, found and named this well. Do you remember Hagar's grief? Compelled to bear a son to Abraham in the face of Sarah's barrenness, she was despised as soon as she conceived. Sarah treated her with harshness and cruelty. Her masters, because of their own lack of faith, used her. When she gave them what they wanted, she was despised. When Sarah finally conceived and Isaac was born, Hagar's son, Ishmael, was rejected and driven out of the family. She had a tough lot in life.

The first time that Sarah mistreated Hagar and she fled from Sarah's presence into the wilderness, Genesis 16:7 tells us that "*the Lord found her.*" Oh, I love it! If the Lord *found* Hagar, it meant that He had noticed that she was gone. He noticed her absence and her loss. He cared about her loss. If He found her, it means that He had been looking for her. She didn't know it, but the search was on; and He didn't give up until He found her by the well of Lahai Roi. She saw Him there, and she said, "*This is the well of Him that lives and sees me*" (see Gen. 16:13-14).

Years later, on the heels of loss, Isaac came from that same well. In a season of death, Isaac clung to the One who lived and saw him.

Before we leave Hagar and continue with Isaac's response, let me comment about the Lord's heart for His hurting daughters. Probably the most tender study in the Bible is the study of God's heart of compassion and love for his daughters who are sad and broken. Think of some of the women in Scripture and the Lord's response to their plights.

Sarah. Barren. *"And the Lord visited Sarah as He had said, and the Lord did for Sarah as He had spoken. For Sarah conceived..."* (Gen. 21:1-2).

Rebekah. Barren. *"And Isaac pleaded with the Lord for his wife... and Rebekah his wife conceived"* (Gen. 25:21).

Leah. Rejected. *"When the Lord saw that Leah was unloved, He opened her womb"* (Gen. 29:31).

Rachel. Barren. *"Then God remembered Rachel, and God listened to her and opened her womb"* (Gen. 30:22).

Hannah. Barren and tormented by her adversary. *"...Hannah conceived"* (1 Sam. 1:20).

Ruth. Bereaved and widowed, she was redeemed by Boaz (whose name means *"strength is in him"*). See the Book of Ruth.

Naomi. Bereaved of two sons and her husband. How real was she in her grief? She said, *"The Almighty has dealt very bitterly with me. I went out full, and the Lord has brought me home again empty"* (Ruth 1:20-21). Nowhere in the Book of Ruth can you find a rebuke from the Lord for Naomi. In fact, the reverse is true. At one point in the story, Boaz (a type of Jesus) says to Ruth, *"It has been fully reported to me, all that you have done for your mother-in-law"* (Ruth 2:11). He was fully aware of her plight and he said to Ruth, *"Do not go empty-handed to your mother-in-law"* (Ruth 3:17). Essentially, Boaz said, "She's had enough loss. She won't return empty any more." At the story's end, the women of the city spoke to Naomi and they said, *"Blessed be the Lord, who has not left you this day without a close relative...and may he be to you a restorer of life and a nourisher of your old age"* (Ruth 4:14-15).

How about the Proverbs 31 woman? Wasn't she perfect? After 14 verses that expound her virtues, verse 25 says, *"She shall rejoice in time to come."* A part of her heart wasn't rejoicing, but it would *in time to come.*

Elizabeth. Barren. *"This is now the sixth month for her who was called barren"* (Lk. 1:36).

Mary. Frightened. *"He has regarded the lowly state of His maid-servant"* (Lk. 1:48).

Jeremiah says that Rachel wept for her children and refused to be comforted. He never rebuked Rachel. His response to her was to say, "Okay. Now no more tears. Your children *will* return." See Jeremiah 31:15-16.

Isaac's journey from Lahai Roi helps to remind us that the Lord remembered Hagar, and He will remember every one of His precious daughters.

Lahai Roi was located between Kadesh (consecrated/set apart) and Bered (greeting) in the south country. South is often representative of blessing in Scripture. Lahai Roi was in a set apart place where the Lord wanted to reintroduce Himself to Isaac. He greeted him kindly and blessed him in the same place where He had revealed Himself to Hagar a generation earlier.

There is a time after loss when tender comfort is needed. Isaac didn't lie down and die and neglect his duties, but he did take time to receive comfort.

Genesis 24:63 says that *"Isaac went out to meditate in the field in the evening."* He meditated and prayed *in the evening.* During grief, certain times will be more poignant than others will. At the poignant times, he meditated on the size of God. He drank deeply of the revelation that God saw him, and he prayed. Pray during the poignant times.

We probably shouldn't be surprised that it was here, in the desert, at night, while praying through his pain, that Isaac first saw Rebekah. She slipped from the camel's back, and he instantly loved her.

Genesis 24:67 says that he brought her into his tent and that he was *"comforted after his mother's death."* The word *comforted* is our word that paints the graphic picture of a mouth-to-mouth resuscitation. It literally means to draw the breath forcibly. Finally, after a prolonged season of grief, Isaac had new life breathed into his spirit from the Lord.

Genesis 25:20 says Isaac was 40 years old when he took Rebekah as his wife. Do you remember that Isaac was 37 when Sarah died? It was *three years* after Sarah's death, before Isaac was finally comforted. I'm not saying that Isaac was in the throes of hard grief for three straight years, but that even after three years, he was still in need of a visitation from God in the area of his grief.

Genesis 25:1 says Abraham (after three years) took another wife. It was three years for Abraham's recovery too. Did the new wife replace Sarah? No. Sarah was still gone, but there was new love.

Did you know that King David also required three years before healing came fully into his soul after the bereavement of his son Ammon?

Please don't be troubled by 30 days and three years. Your season could be longer or shorter. The pattern we should follow from Abraham and Isaac is simply this:

1. **Grieve.** Grieve hard.

2. **Purchase Machpelah.** Grieve with hope and understanding, carefully selecting the resting-place

for your grief. Remember, that even through loss (subtraction), the Lord can double the anointing in your life.

3. **Eventually begin moving.** Be accountable with your grief and don't allow a spiritual hypothermia to settle over your soul.

4. **Never forget that the Lord is eternally gentle with His daughters.**

5. **Remember: the Lord will visit you again.**

6. **Practice prayer during the poignant times.**

7. **Be assured: comfort will come.** New breath will enter your spirit, even if it takes three years to get there.

Randy Becton in *Everyday Comfort* quoted Dr. William Worden, a grief counselor, and offered a similar pattern for the recovery from grief. He wrote:

> Dr. William Worden spoke recently on "When is mourning finished?" His guidelines indicate there are no easy answers, but he offered these encouragements:

> No one can set the time, but in the loss of a close loved one, full resolution through grief probably occurs within two years. One indicator of recovery is the ability to think of the loved one without great pain, only with a sweet sadness. Another indicator of recovery is that time when you can re-invest your emotions into living. Some studies have shown that three to four years must pass before emotional pain has gone. Watch for the way you respond when friends mention your loved one. You will see how well you are adjusting. Your loss is a permanent part of your life.[14]

My dear friends, go ahead and grieve. Go ahead and weep and wail and be very, very honest and real. However, remember that He is coming and that He promises to dry tears for eternity. Your tragedy cannot dim His plan for your life. He still desires to know you and to use you.

The biblical response to grief in a nutshell can be found in Psalm 69:32, "*You who seek God, your hearts shall live.*" The Holy Spirit acknowledges that there are times when our hearts feel dead and we wonder if we will ever live again. He doesn't rebuke us. He simply says, "I'm still here. Seek Me. I loved bringing Isaac his wife in the desert. The camels are still coming." Your heart will live that seeks God! He will help you.

He will respond to your grief!

6

A Dangerous Intersection

Life is full of intersections. Some merely provide alternate routes to the same destination. Others determine destiny. Some can be navigated by simply slowing down. Others screech us to a halt.

There are crossroads of moral seduction when we're tempted to turn aside from our vows of fidelity. There are crossroads of financial integrity when we must decide to choose honesty above crooked opportunity.

All relationships come to inevitable crossroads where the wills of the members of the relationship collide. The question looms, "Will I lay my life down for the one I love, or will I demand my own rights?"

There are crossroads that tempt compromise in every area of ethical integrity. The direction we turn at these intersections reveals our character. These particular intersections will either make us or break us.

One of the deadliest intersections we will ever face comes to us on the heels of seemingly unanswered prayer. Great confusion can set in when we have taken God at His word only to come up short of a miracle. When we've done our best to stand on what we think He's told us and yet we don't get the expected results, it can catapult us into a crossroad of confusion. The confusion settles in around the fact that *we thought we had heard His voice.*

This is the place where our faith intersects with loss. It's that part of the highway where our confident expectation meets brutal reality. It's that place where we're tempted to veer off the road.

I have a friend who is sitting at such a crossroad. Many years ago, he became convinced that God was leading him onto a specific career path. He bought the farm (in a manner of speaking) and changed careers in midstream. Committing to his new profession, his hopes were high, and his family was rejoicing in anticipation of the blessings that the Lord had promised them.

Unfortunately, things didn't work out. A year after taking this step of faith, they had seen little fruit, no significant blessings, and they were contemplating bankruptcy.

What happened? Did they miss God? Were they acting out of presumption? Certainly God didn't mislead them, did He? They're now parked at a crossroad.

Has your life ever stalled at an intersection like this one?

Mine has.

I just knew that God had spoken to me in the neo-natal intensive care unit on the day of Alexis' birth. It had to be God!

I was huddled over her incubator watching the respirator assist her breathing while numerous machines monitored her blood pressure, heart rate, and oxygen saturation. She had an i.v. protruding from her little forehead. She was tiny and frail and gorgeous. A kind nurse had just given me a cloth diaper as my tears flowed unchecked. My heart was dying, and fear was terrorizing my soul. That's when I heard it. *"Pursue, for you shall surely overtake them and without fail recover all."*

It was the Scripture verse that I had been reading the evening before. Where did it come from? I wasn't thinking about King David's plight at Ziklag as I watched Alexis fight for her first few breaths. The devil would never encourage me to fight for a miracle. It had to be God! I knew it was God. It was biblical. It came unbidden into my consciousness right when I needed to hear it. And it gave me peace.

Crying in the nursery, the Word of the Lord exploded in my soul, and I experienced a new reality amidst the choking grip of fear—faith.

"Faith comes by hearing, and hearing by the word of God" (Rom. 10:17). I heard a word and faith rose to meet it. Alexis needed a miracle, but God had countered her need with a word. "Pursue." If I pursued, Alexis would recover. Simple.

To this day, I don't believe I missed God. I don't believe my desperate father's heart played a trick on my mind that evening in the NICU. I don't believe satan deceived me.

God spoke to me! Only He could have pierced my suffocating despair and aroused a warrior's heart in me. Only He could have sustained our three-year fight. Only He could have brought people to the Lord as a result of Alexis' condition.

Only He can explain to me why she wasn't healed.

To navigate the crossroad of unanswered prayer, we must recognize that **some questions have no answers on this side of eternity.** I'm so sorry to tell you that! I wish that I could explain why your loved one has made certain choices. I wish I could explain why your fasting hasn't seemed to work like you thought it would. I'm sure you've done everything you know to do in pursuit of your blessing—I wish I could make sense of it all.

All I can do is offer to hold a place in line for you in Heaven. You know the line I'm referencing, don't you? It's the line of people wanting to ask those tough questions of the Lord.

I used to say that I'm going to cut to the front of the line when I get to Heaven so I can ask Him why bad things happen to good people. I want to know why some people get healed and other people don't. I want to know why certain prayers are answered and others aren't. I really want to ask those questions.

I have a suspicion, though.

If I stand in line long enough, beholding His beauty, I'll probably forget my questions. I'll probably fall at His feet. I'll beg Him to hold me tight. I'll realize that He has always been sovereign and that He has always loved me.

He's always loved *you*! Even when your prayer seemed to go unanswered.

Will you come to Heaven with me? Can I show you some things that happen there?

When John the Beloved was exiled on the Island of Patmos, he saw a door standing open in Heaven. A voice issued from the door saying, *"Come up here, and I will show you things which must take place..."* (Rev. 4:1).

Can I be that voice for just a moment? Can I show you what will take place someday in Heaven? Using imagination and insights from Revelation 7, let me paint the scene.

There are thousands and thousands of people. They're wearing white—dazzling white. Palm branches are in their hands. They are beautiful.

There are men, women, and children from every imaginable race. Some are black, and some are white. Some are Asian, and some are Hispanic. They look like God!

They're speaking, but their speech can't be deciphered because they are each speaking in their native tongue. It's awesome! French is blending with Russian, which is mingling with Japanese, which is getting covered up by Crow Indian.

They form a living, breathing human tapestry. Their national, redemptive gifts are on display before the king, and their speech sounds like waterfalls and songbirds and thunder. Their roar of worship crescendos, and suddenly you can understand them. They're singing, "Salvation belongs to our God who sits on the throne!"

Angels join the worship as elders begin dropping their crowns and falling before the throne. They're singing, "Amen, blessing and glory and wisdom and thanksgiving and honor and power and might, be to our God forever and ever!"

Then you ask a question: "Who are these who are clothed in the white robes?"

An elder looks up from the floor and responds, "They are those who have come out of great tribulation. The tribulation that they endured was so severe that it crushed them. You have no English word that matches the intensity of the crushing. A Greek word, *thlipsis*, comes close. *Thlipsis* describes that force of pressure that cracks, breaks, crumbles, and crushes anything that comes near it. A visual picture of the word's intensity would be that of an object being forced through a tube that is diminishing in diameter. The farther through the tube the object goes, the greater the pressure increases upon it. Eventually the pressure becomes too great, and the object fractures, splinters, and is ground into powder. This is the type of tribulation that these saints have endured. They've been broken. They've been crushed.

"There is something you must know about them, however. In their tribulation, they never grew bitter. Instead, they washed themselves in the blood of the Lamb. They clung to King Jesus. They have made it a practice to stand before His throne. In fact, they never leave. Day or night, you can find them standing before Him, serving Him, worshipping Him.

"An awesome thing has happened to them as they've stood before Him. He has spread the covering of His presence over them. When you look at them, you're not really seeing them— you're seeing Him. The white radiance of their robes is actually a reflection of His glory shining on them. They're hidden in Him. They're safe.

"I've been watching them for a long time now. I've been here in Heaven for untold centuries, and I've seen wonders to pale all dreams. However, I'm most intrigued by a simple mystery that transpires every day.

"Every day, the King steps down from His throne. He becomes a shepherd, and He leads these particular saints to the springs of the water of life.

"He bathes them there. He heals them. He talks to them. He answers their questions. One by one, morning after morning, I see Him wiping away their tears. They've cried a lot. Their tribulation almost destroyed them, but they're here, in His presence; and every morning, they drink together from the water of life. It undoes me every day. All I can do is cast my crown in the dust, fall to my knees, and cry, 'Holy!' He loves them so much!

"I've learned a lot from watching the Shepherd-King with His saints. I've learned that the questions that haunt mankind on planet Earth don't matter as much here. I've learned that He always makes sense out of their loose ends in time. His passion is to take His saints to the springs of the water of life. He wants them to drink deeply.

"I've learned something else too. He doesn't want them to wait until they get to Heaven to taste this water. It's available to them on Earth.

"While on planet Earth, as a man, Jesus once said, 'If any man is thirsty, let him come to Me and drink.' Jesus is the source of living water, and He beckons to His hurting ones to drink deeply of His healing love."

This moving speech has stirred you to your core. Desperate to be led by your Shepherd to the source of life you cry out, "Sir, how can I meet Him in this place?" His simple answer echoes through your soul: "Pray! Prayer is the pathway to living water."

Heaven fades, and you're suddenly back on earth.

"Prayer?" you say. "Prayer is the answer? Prayer feels nothing like a plunge in living water. I'm hurting, and I'm being strangled by my questions. Prayer is hard. When I pray, I hear few answers. I'm receiving little guidance. Prayer, if anything, is a reminder that I didn't receive my miracle."

And suddenly, you see it. You're standing at a crossroad. You realize that this is a defining moment. Your destiny could be determined right here. Four roads diverge at your feet. They are not unattractive paths. They are actually quite appealing. In fact, unknowingly, your feet have already started to veer off course.

You've stepped into the crossroad of confusion. It's a normal place to find yourself in the aftermath of great struggle.

The finality of loss can bring confusion to our prayer lives. The person who is standing in faith for an unbelieving spouse knows how to pray. "God, save him! God, deliver him! God, capture his heart! God, hold me while I stand."

But what if divorce occurs? What if they've done all to stand and their spouse made the wrong decision? Now, how do they pray? Prayer can be a perplexing thing to a soul in pain.

So can Bible reading.

After Alexis' death, my wife and I responded very differently in our spiritual disciplines. I loved to read the Bible! It brought peace and hope to my heart, and it acted like healing ointment for the rupture in my soul. I clung to the Word as the only lifeline that was sure.

On the other hand, I couldn't pray. I didn't trust that I could hear from the Lord, and I didn't know what to say.

Jessica responded in the opposite manner. Worship saved her. She clung to prayer. While, for me, prayer was a hollow, impotent ritual, for her it was life. She worshiped! She prayed!

Many times I would return home from work to the sound of blaring worship music and her passionate declarations that arose from the desperate state of her soul. Thank God she prayed!

Where she struggled was with the Word. Accounts of miracles and healings rang in her ears like a cruel mockery.

Well, He's healing her.

This very morning, before I left for the office, Jessica said, "Let me share with you some insights I've been getting from the Word."

He's healing me too. Somehow I've finally learned to pray again.

I still cry at times, though. Last weekend I watched Disney's *Finding Nemo* with Amber and Madelyn. (For those of you who don't watch children's movies, I'll elaborate.) *Finding Nemo* is the story of a fish's quest to find his son, Nemo, who was taken by a diver and placed in an aquarium in a dental office. Nemo's father, Marlin, is a timid, little clown fish (Nemo's mother, brothers, and sisters were all killed by a shark) who embarks on an epic adventure to rescue Nemo.

The scene that reduced me to tears was when word of Marlin's great pursuit began to spread through the entire ocean. A turtle told a seahorse who told a crab who told a swordfish who told a dolphin who told a pelican who eventually told Nemo in the dentist's office. He said, "Your dad has crossed the whole ocean looking for you! I heard he took on three sharks and that he's on his way here right now!"

It broke me. The little clown fish faced sharks, jellyfish, and whales as he searched for his son. He faced mockery, self-doubt, and despair. I don't know how else to say it, except that I felt like Marlin. I felt like I swam an ocean—although I never found the miracle.

Stopped in my tracks, confusion clouding my reasoning, I see I have entered a crossroad of unanswered prayer. Prayer got me here. Can it really be that prayer must carry me through to the other side?

I'm not the best pray-er in the world. I'm not sure I even know what to say. Somehow I think that's okay.

Hannah didn't know how to pray either. Do you remember Hannah and her prayer? Barren and tormented by her adversary, she poured out her soul to the Lord only to be rebuked by the priest. Eli saw her at the altar and thought she was drunk. Hannah shows us that prayer is not the proper recitation of eloquent words but a simple heart cry offered honestly to the Lord. Let's listen in. I think Eli's speaking with her right now.

I Am Not Drunk—I'm Simply Trying to Pray!

"You're drunk! How long will you remain in this state? Put away your wine and quit defiling the altar of the Lord!"

"Oh, no, my lord, I am not drunk. I've had neither wine nor strong drink. Please don't consider me a worthless woman."

"Then tell me, what is the state of your soul? For you utter words but no sound issues forth."

"I'm trying to pray, but the words catch in my throat. I know my lips are moving, but I can barely make a sound. I'm hurting. My heart is chained in the irons of a slave. It's a cruel and bitter yoke that has been placed upon my soul. I fear I cannot bear it!"

"What are you doing here?"

"I've been pouring out my soul to the Lord. I'm spilling the contents of my innermost being out before Him. What else can I do? I'm not hiding anything from Him. I have no fear of His scrutiny. I need Him! If God doesn't come through, I am as frail and lost as a condemned man upon a cross. No, sir, I am not drunk. I'm simply trying to pray. It's just that the words aren't coming out."

Do you remember the story? Here's the precise reading from Scripture.

So Hannah arose after they had finished eating and drinking in Shiloh. Now Eli the priest was sitting on the seat by the doorpost of the tabernacle of the Lord. And she was in bitterness of soul, and prayed to the Lord and wept in anguish. Then she made a vow and said, "O Lord of hosts, if You will indeed look on the affliction of Your maidservant and remember me, and not forget Your maidservant, but will give Your maidservant a male child, then I will give him to the Lord all the days of his life, and no razor shall come upon his head." And it happened, as she continued praying before the Lord, that Eli watched her mouth. **Now Hannah spoke in her heart; only her lips moved, but her voice was not heard.** *Therefore Eli thought she was drunk. So Eli said to her, "How long will you be drunk? Put your wine away from you!" But Hannah answered and said, "No, my lord, I am a woman of sorrowful spirit. I have drunk neither wine nor intoxicating drink, but have poured out my soul before the Lord. Do not consider your maidservant a wicked woman, for out of the abundance of my complaint and grief I have spoken until now"* (1 Samuel 1:9-16, emphasis added).

Hannah prayed until she could pray no more. She prayed until the words stopped flowing. She simply prayed from her heart. I should mention, in case you've forgotten, that the Lord heard her voiceless prayer. Eli blessed her. She conceived. Samuel was her son. Do you remember that the Scripture says that Samuel's words never fell to the ground? Perhaps that's because Hannah felt like hers did.

Your prayers haven't fallen to the ground either. Continue to offer Him your heart's cry. He can handle it, and you need to express it. Pray!

7

Reaching Nirvana

There's a danger for those who are weary from great struggle. They have a genuine need for some happiness. They have a genuine need to experience the abundant life. However, they need to be careful to look for it in the right place.

I preached a sermon a couple years ago entitled, "Reaching Nirvana." I wasn't trying to convert our congregation to Buddhism, but I was pointing out the fact that many Christians act and think like practicing Buddhists. Let me explain.

I was experiencing one of the strange paradoxes of life. Madelyn had been born just a week earlier, and although I felt intense joy at her birth, I was wrestling with some inner distress that didn't make sense. I was thrilled to have another healthy daughter. I already loved her with every cell of my being. My marriage was wonderful, and our church was growing and thriving. So why was I struggling? I didn't feel any particular grief regarding Alexis. I was happy.

And I was sad.

I was at a Barnes and Nobel bookstore, randomly perusing new book titles, as I pondered the strange contrast of emotions in my soul. While I walked and thought and prayed, I approached the eastern religions section, and I became intrigued with the titles of numerous books written by the Dalai Lama. They were great topics. Listen to some of them: *The Art of Happiness, The*

Compassionate Life, The Good Heart, Healing Anger, How to Practice the Way to a Meaningful Life, The Way to Freedom, An Open Heart, The Path to Tranquility and Ethics for a New Millennium. Great titles! They appealed to me.

I wanted to know the art of happiness. I wanted to live a compassionate and meaningful life. I realized there in the bookstore that, although I was a Christian and a minister, I was missing some of the abundant life. Then it dawned on me. After a lifetime of practicing Christianity, I was thinking like a Buddhist.

The opening line from the Dali Lama's *The Art of Happiness* says this: "I believe that the very purpose of our life is to seek happiness." That mind-set permeates the Buddhist religion. Buddhists cling to their three jewels, their four noble truths, and their cardinal precepts all with the hope of someday reaching the happiness of nirvana.

What is *nirvana*? Its definition might surprise you. Part of it sounds like something out of the Bible. *Nirvana* is the peace that passes understanding. Once reached, it is the state of being in the world, but not of the world. It is the state of perfection where all suffering is extinguished. It is the highest bliss and the end of mortal anguish. The ultimate state of nirvana is death.

Why am I interrupting our talk on prayer with this Buddhist tangent? Because Buddhists are looking for happiness. So are Christians. So are you. You need some happiness. You need to experience some joy. I do too. The problem is that Buddhists are deceived, and sadly, so are many Christians.

Christianity is not the means to a happy life. Christianity, as a religion alone, has no more life than Buddhism. Christianity is the means to a relationship with Jesus Christ. Happiness is a by-product of that relationship. If our Christian disciplines are not bringing us deeper into a relationship with Jesus, we are as lost as those sincere Buddhists who are struggling to break free from samsara (the endless cycles of arduous life).

Christians shouldn't be looking for life. We already possess it in abundance. Do you feel like you do? Are you experiencing it? If not, it's possible that your life's struggles have made you forget the mystery that *God is within the believer.* New Agers make that sound like heresy. The apostle Paul said it was a mystery. He said *"...Christ in you, the hope of glory"* (Col. 1:27 NASB).

Christ in me. Wow! Do I feel like He's in me? Not very often. Usually I feel empty and in desperate need of Him.

Christ in you. Do you feel His indwelling presence? Do you feel His joy? Do you feel His victory? Do you know that Jesus is happy? He's at peace! He has absorbed your pain and your sin and your sorrow, and He is victorious forever. And *He is in you.*

I'd like to submit a thought to you. I don't believe that the average Christian prays from this mysterious perspective. I think they pray like Buddhists.

Hear me out! We talk about prayer. We offer up prayers. We say our prayers. We use prayer as a means to get Heaven, to move in our situations so we can experience more happiness. However, we have a problem. We've forgotten the mystery, and consequently, prayer has become our external attempt to connect with God.

God is not looking to facilitate an external meeting with us. He's already *in* us. Perfect peace is already in you. Victory is already in you. Freedom from sin is already in you. The healing you need from your disappointment is already in you.

I believe that only a minute fraction of Christians have discovered the reality of the truth and power that is resident in that simple verse from Colossians. "Christ in you is the hope of glory."

Colossians is a great book of victory. It contains three primary concepts:

1. Christ is in us.

2. Satan has been made a public display of humiliation and defeat.

3. We are complete in Jesus.

If we miss that first revelation that Christ is in us, we will miss the note of victory, and we will find Colossians to be a book of depression, sorrow, and failure. We will feel that we, not satan, have been made a public spectacle, and we will feel powerless to please God and fulfill His commands in our lives.

Let's walk through some verses from Colossians together, and then I will share a simple prayer with you that can be of vital significance in your healing process.

Colossians 3:3 says, "*For you have died and your life is hidden with Christ in God* (NASB)." What a statement! For you have died. There is no hidden meaning in these words. There's no other way to interpret them. They simply mean that you're dead.

You and I are dead. We're dead in sin. We're dead in our attempts to fulfill the law. We're dead in our attempts to find happiness. (Solomon had far more resources at his disposal to pursue happiness than us, and yet he concluded that apart from relationship with God, all was vanity, futility, and death.) We are dead in our attempts to find Jesus and live a successful Christian life. (Remember that Christianity is the record of God's pursuit of mankind, not man's pursuit of God.) The bottom line is that we are dead.

We're dead, and our life is hidden with Christ in God. It's great that our life is with God, but sometimes we don't know where to find Him. Even if we thought we could find Him, we still doubt that we would find life. It's hidden.

Verse 4 says, "*When Christ, who is our life, is revealed, then you also will be revealed with Him in glory*." A major error often occurs in our understanding at this point in the text. Most people interpret the phrase, "*When Christ...is revealed* (NASB)," to mean when He returns in the second coming. When Jesus is revealed—whenever that is—we'll be revealed with Him. We innocently assume that His (and our) revealing await a future date, and we end up completely missing the point and the revelation of the verse.

From a dead place, and with the false understanding that our glory and life are waiting a future event for their revealing, we read verse 5, "*Therefore consider the members of your earthly body as dead to immorality, impurity, passion, evil desire, and greed, which amounts to idolatry* (NASB)." Following this verse are six more verses that list the evils of various sins and exhort us to forsake them.

Then it gets worse. We know we're dead. We assume that His glory is postponed. We have a whole list of things we shouldn't do. Then we get three verses of great Christ-like attributes that we should exemplify.

Then we read verse 15 that says, "*And* [as if all of the above was not enough] *let the peace of Christ rule* [*rule* means to govern or prevail] *in your hearts* (NASB)." We agree with that! We want the peace of Christ to prevail in our hearts instead of anxiety, stress, fear, and discouragement. *Peace* here is the Greek word *eirene*, and it means an untroubled, undisturbed state of well-being.

We want that, but how do we get it? We're beginning to break. We think, I'm dead and I'm doing my best—from this place of the dead—to resist sin and be like Christ. I'm trying to live the abundant life of Christ from a place of death. I know I'll have a mansion on a hill in Heaven, but here on Earth, I'm camped out in a cemetery.

Verses 16-17 give a little hope because they sound at first to be a strategy.

Let the word of Christ richly dwell within you, with all wisdom teaching and admonishing one another with psalms and hymns and spiritual songs, singing with thankfulness in your hearts to God. And Whatever you do in word or deed, do all in the name of the Lord Jesus, giving thanks through Him to God the Father (NASB).

These are great keys:

1. The Word of God.

2. Accountability.

3. Praise and worship.

4. Thankfulness.

5. The pursuit of excellence in my calling.

Great! Here's a strategy. That's what I've been looking for. There's only one problem. I'm still dead. Maybe I should keep reading.

The next five verses bury me. I've just found some more mandates. I'm trying to forsake sin, embrace righteousness, practice the spiritual disciplines, and become excellent in my calling. Now I'm told to be a great, Christ-like husband? I'm supposed to be an exemplary father? I also need to serve my employer as if I was serving Jesus Himself? I'm sinking. Remember, when I started all this, I was already dead.

In verses 23-24, we are again admonished to pursue excellence. Since that was important enough to be stated twice, I'd better get a little more focused on this particular point. I'd better go to a conference. I'd better read some books. I'd better set some goals. I'll do my best.

Verse 25 concludes the chapter with, "*For he who does wrong will receive the consequences of the wrong which he has done, and that without partiality* (NASB)." Oh, my! I'd better not fail. Honestly, though, I have very little hope of succeeding in any of the above-mentioned mandates, let alone all of them. Remember, I'm dead. I guess I'd better get busy, but I'm starting to sink. Depression is settling in. I'm overwhelmed. Oh yeah, then there's the devil.

He's still waltzing around like a hungry lion. I need to make sure to resist him firm in the faith. Okay. Let's get started.

Sadly, that commentary is a typical description of the life of a dutiful saint. Doing his best to witness to the world, this saint secretly wonders, *What is different about my life? Do I really have anything that the world would want? I know, of course, that I have my eternal salvation and that's worth all the struggle, so I'll try to carry on. I just wish I could experience a little more of the abundant life. Then again, perhaps that's just reserved for Heaven. After all, I need to stay "seated with Christ in heavenly places."*

All of these very honest thoughts are compounded in seasons of disappointment and heartache. However, we've missed the entire point. Our life is not reserved for some future end-time event. It's here right now—it's just that it's hidden with Christ in God. We have it. We only need to surrender fully to Him to access it.

I know what you might be saying. "I don't want that to be the answer! I don't want the answer to be surrender. Surrender to Jesus. Die to the flesh. Yield to Him. Will I still be a Christian if I confess that at this point in my life, the thought of that produces a loathing in me? Surrender fully to Christ and let Him live His life through me. That sounds so painful, so hard, so miserable, and so boring. I'm already hurting so badly that I don't know if I can surrender anymore. I'm afraid that if I truly surrender everything to Him, I won't have a life. He'll either send me to Africa, or He'll constantly ask me to witness to everyone I meet. I won't be able to have fun because I'll constantly be convicted. I'll have to spend all my time praying or reading the Bible. I do love God, but I just wish that weren't the answer. I'm hurting and I'm weary, and I wish there were another way. Is something wrong with me?"

No. It's just that you've come full circle. After all this time, you've never made it out of Genesis chapter 3. You're standing where Eve stood; you're holding the fruit, and you're facing the serpent. The serpent is talking. In fact, he just keeps repeating himself. He's lying to you! Just like he lied to Eve. He's very good at it. He convinced Eve that God was holding out on her—that a life of surrender to His will would rob her of happiness. He's almost got you convinced too. I think you should run. Run back to Colossians 3:3.

It says, "*For you have died and your life is hidden with Christ in God*" (emphasis added). If your life is hidden, it means that you have some life. What kind of life is it? Paul said it was *zoe* life. *Zoe* is the highest blessedness that Christ is and gives to His saints. *Zoe* is the highest blessedness of the creature. It is life like we've never known before. It's joy unspeakable. It's peace that surpasses all understanding. It's hope that flourishes despite catastrophe. It's faith that is unmoved by cruel facts. It is laughter that begins from your toes and rushes through your whole body like a spring torrent. It is satisfaction. It is rest. It is purpose. It is all that makes life worth living. It is life.

However, it's hidden. You can't find it. *Hidden* means to veil or cover or conceal. You know that life exists; but there's a veil separating you from it, and that's what causes your desperation. You were made for life, but you're dead. You were created for a garden, but you live in a desert. You are eternal, but you exist in a dying body. You know you were made for life so you set out in a frantic pursuit. I wonder, though, have you asked directions for how to find it? Or are you just doing your best to fulfill the mandates of Colossians chapter 3?

I have a message for you. The abundant life is hidden from you, and you won't find it in verses 5-25. It's not just hidden randomly; it's hidden *with Christ*.

So where is He?

He's in you.

Verse 4 says, "*When Christ...our life, is revealed, then you also will be revealed with Him in glory.*" Revealed means to take the lid off. Zoe has been hidden and covered, but Jesus will take the lid off.

Life, although hidden, is already inside you. The only way to access it is to allow Christ to be revealed in you. When Christ is revealed, then you also will be revealed.

Our purpose or goal can never be to discover ourselves (our gifts, callings, etc). Our purpose must be to reveal Him through us. When He is revealed in us, then we will be revealed. When people see Jesus in you, they'll see the real you. When you allow Him to live through you, you'll live again.

True life will never be found in any other place but Jesus. True life will never be lived until Jesus is living His life through us. The serpent may scream at us, but the serpent is destined for hell. You are destined for life. Jesus is life. The only way to find life is to find Jesus. I didn't say to fulfill Colossians 3:5-25. I said to find Jesus.

I hope this all makes sense. Remember, it's a mystery. It's hard to believe and understand on our best days. It's even harder when we don't feel His presence on our worst days.

Jesus is the source of living water. Prayer is the pathway to get there. Jesus dwells within you. Prayer and surrender release Him through you.

I know this is easier said than done. The next chapter will be more helpful. Before we get there, though, can we pray together?

Sweet Jesus, I thank You that You have chosen me for Your own. Thank You for allowing me to be a part of Your temple on earth. I need You today! I need the life and peace and joy and healing that only You can supply. I release You to live Your life through me. I renounce the taunting voice of my adversary. I strangle the serpent in Jesus' name! By faith, I release the river of living water that You've placed within me. Please heal me and allow Your peace to surpass my understanding. Would You bypass my intellect and my questioning heart and let Your life reign. I love You, and I will cling to You all the days of my life. Despite my confusion and my pain, I ask You to have Your way in me. I don't want to pursue happiness—I want to pursue You. I want to know Jesus. I want to know His life. I want Him to laugh through me again. I want to feel His faith. Help me to embrace this. Help me to live it. I am forever Yours! Amen.

8

Will You Be Made Whole?

A strange, yet wonderful phenomena had broken out in a church in Spokane when Alexis was almost three years old. This church experienced an outpouring from God where, during the services, people's dental fillings turned to gold.

I took Alexis to a healing service that this church was hosting in hope that the Lord might touch her in a special way. This hope-filled evening became one of the darkest nights of my time with Alexis. Let me explain.

Alexis had a seizure disorder that mandated the use of significant amounts of the drugs Phenobarbital and Klonopin. While the drugs helped minimize the seizures, they also had the sad effect of thickening her gums. Since she was fed through a feeding tube in her stomach, she didn't have the ability to cut her teeth on chew toys and food items. This lack of oral stimulation, combined with the side effect from the seizure medication, created quite a problem for her. Instead of teething and drooling and whining like other babies and eventually smiling with a toothy grin, her gums became terribly swollen and painful. Her teeth pressed painfully against her gums but were unable to break through because of the thickening effect of the seizure meds.

After we spent weeks massaging multiple tubes of oragel throughout her little mouth, a pediatric dentist performed a surgery that allowed her teeth to emerge. He used an electro-surge device to cut a thin line into her gums to relieve the swelling and pressure. When he did this, Alexis immediately experienced relief, and her little teeth showed through. However, the surgery left her gums blackened and scarred. They eventually healed, and the seizure meds became less of a problem for her; but it was in the early stages of recovery from this oral surgery when her gums were hurting and raw, that I took her to this special healing service. I wish I hadn't.

The service was wonderful. The worship was sweet, and the presence of the Lord was strong. Then it began to happen.

All around me people began shouting and staring into one another's open mouths as fillings, literally, turned to gold. It was real! I even stole a peek at an ecstatic young man who was sitting beside me and saw bright, shining, gold fillings in his gaping mouth. On most other days, I probably would have whooped and hollered and shouted, "Hallelujah" with the best of them. This night, however, all I could do was cry.

A member from the altar ministry team came over and prayed a distracted prayer over Alexis, and then told me I should let her soak in this great anointing. I realize even as I write this that I sound bitter. I am not. The Lord was genuinely touching some of the people there that night, but I just couldn't understand why He would turn a perfectly good filling to gold and overlook a three-year-old who was hurting from her blackened and swollen gums. I left early, and I cried the whole way home. I cried myself to sleep.

I really needed the Lord to speak to me, but when He did, it wasn't what I expected. I thought He would bring comfort and be a very present help in my trouble. Instead, He asked me a question. "Will you be made whole?" What a strange question it was for such a dark moment in my soul. I'm so glad He asked it, however, because it changed my life. I hope I answered it correctly.

Will you be made whole? It's a very simple question, but it demands an answer. The Lord asked it in John 5, and He is asking it today. He's asking it of you. He's asking you, "Will you be made whole?" He's asking this because He loves you so much, and He doesn't want you to live forever in the throes of grief-induced sorrow.

Will you be made whole? Sometimes I have to answer, "I have no clue, Lord. You alone know."

It's a very tender question. It's not a condemning question, and it's not a rhetorical one either. If we answer it correctly, we can receive some wholeness. In an earlier chapter, He asked us why we were crying. In this chapter, let's evaluate this text and extract some keys that will help us answer the question: "Will you be made whole?"

John the beloved disciple tells the story. John 5:1-9 says,

After this there was a feast of the Jews; and Jesus went up to Jerusalem. Now there is at Jerusalem by the sheep market a pool, which is called in the Hebrew tongue Bethesda, having five porches. In these lay a great multitude of impotent folk, of blind, halt, withered, waiting for the moving of the water. For an angel went down at a certain season into the pool, and troubled the water: whosoever then first after the troubling of the water stepped in was made whole of whatsoever disease he had. And a certain man was there, which had an infirmity thirty and eight years. When Jesus saw him lie, and knew that he had been now a long time in that case, He saith unto him, Wilt thou be made whole? The impotent man answered him, Sir, I have no man, when the water is troubled, to put me into the pool: but while I am coming, another steppeth down before me. Jesus saith unto him, Rise, take up thy bed, and walk. And immediately the man was made whole, and took up his bed, and walked: and on the same day was the sabbath (KJV).

Verse 1 says, "*After this.*" After what? What does *this* reference? Our story occurred immediately after Jesus performed a healing for a nobleman's son. Somebody just got a miracle, and when someone else is healed or touched by God, it can be a hard time for the grieving. It's hard, not because we are jealous or spiteful or because we aren't genuinely happy for someone else who is blessed. We *are* happy for them. It just hurts.

After this, there was a feast of the Jews, and Jesus went up to Jerusalem. And there was by the sheep market a pool with five covered colonnades. It was feast time in Jerusalem, and here, beneath the covered colonnades, was a shady area near the temple of God. It sounds nice, doesn't it? It's a shaded pool beside the presence of God. It almost sounds like something out of Psalm 23. There were only a few problems.

This place was also by the sheep market. The sheep market was the place where sheep were bought and sold for sacrifices. This lovely setting was actually a sheep pen. Although at first glance, it looked like a place of peace and rest, it probably smelled like a barn as the hot summer sun cooked the sheep droppings. It's fun to pet the sheep at a county fair, but no one wants to have a picnic in their pen. The pool may sound nice, but it was probably filled with wool clippings, sheep backwash, and its fair share of sheep slime.

"*In these lay a great multitude.*" Sure, it's surrounded by five covered colonnades, but it's still a hot, stinky, slimy place—and it's packed with a great multitude. It's bad enough when you're crowded in a football stadium or a shopping mall, but a sheep pen? It's not even like they were packed in a rodeo or a football stadium where people wanted to be there. Here, everyone had a problem.

"*In these lay a great multitude of impotent people.*" Impotent people. People with no power lay here. The Greek version of our English word *impotent* is *astheo*. *Astheo* is a compound word comprised of *stheo*, which means to strengthen and the negative prefix *a*. The word implies strength with a negative clinging to it. God desired to strengthen some people, but there was negativity clinging to them—especially because they felt impotent.

The Scripture continues the description of these impotent people as *"blind, halt, withered."* Some of the people were physically afflicted. Some were physically blind, halt, and withered; but our Greek definitions inform us that the words also have spiritual ramifications. They were spiritually weak, weak in faith, weak in riches, and destitute of authority.

Some were physically blind; others just had no vision for their life, their family, or the Kingdom of God.

Some were physically lame; others had just given up and quit running.

Some were called "halt" in the KJV translation. Perhaps they had been strong runners, passionately pursuing the things of God, and then, due to disappointments and the circumstances of life, they had come to a halt.

If someone is blind, halt, or lame, you can spot him or her pretty easily. If a man has no vision, he will often carry himself like he is defeated. However, there is also a fourth group listed. The Scripture says that they were also *"waiting for the moving of the water."* Some were in the powerless position of waiting. You may look wonderful on the outside; however, no one would ever know that you're waiting. You're wrestling with secret disappointments. Some of you smiled this morning and chatted jovially with your coworkers, but you're waiting. In seasons of waiting, great distress can come upon us. Seasons of waiting are great revealers of character.

Grosart wrote of waiting:

You remember that strange half-involuntary "forty years" of Moses in the "wilderness" of Midian, when he had fled from Egypt. You remember, too, the almost equally strange years of retirement in "Arabia," by Paul, when, if ever, humanly speaking, instant action was needed. And pre-eminently you remember the amazing charge of the ascending Lord to the disciples, "Tarry at Jerusalem." Speaking after the manner of men, one could not have wondered if out-spoken Peter, or fervid James, had said: "Tarry, Lord! How long?" "Tarry, Lord! is there not a perishing world, groaning for the 'good news?' " "Tarry! did we hear thee aright, Lord? Was the word not haste?" Nay![15]

I wonder how many people look good outwardly, like five covered colonnades beside a pool, but on the inside they are waiting. Waiting makes you feel powerless. Do you see the picture emerging from the text? They're impotent worshippers looking good on the outside. They're waiting. In this story, they were waiting for the "*troubling of the water.*"

It's an amazing story. It seems that an angel would go down at a certain season and stir up the water; and when the water was thus stirred or troubled, a healing power was released into its touch. Whoever was the first one to get into the water would be healed of whatever disease he had. This is a fantastic, mysterious, intriguing story, and I don't doubt that it happened. John didn't seem to question it. He didn't say, "There was a legend that an angel would trouble the water." He simply said it happened. If Jesus had a problem with the story, He certainly could have silenced the rumor. The fact is that an angel entered the pool, and when the water was troubled, healing emerged.

Please notice two things with me here. First, there is no healing in a stagnant pool. To make forward progress in water, you must create waves. If there is no stirring, there is no healing. There is no healing in a stagnant spiritual life either. We'll see in just a moment that if we remain stagnant for too long, we won't be able to answer the question, "Will you be made whole?" Grief promotes stagnation. All enthusiasm and motivation subside when the painful waves of grief capsize the soul. That's normal.

It's okay to lose focus and passion, but remember what we studied in a previous chapter: The healing process requires movement. Don't move rashly or prematurely, but please move. Don't lie down and die. Even after significant physical surgeries, the patients are required to stretch and move. Years ago, physicians didn't understand this principle, and they allowed their patients to lie still for much longer periods of time. Consequently, their convalescence was much slower and more painful. Move.

Second, notice with me that the first to embrace the troubling of the water was made whole. Human nature is to reject the trouble; but if we would embrace it and wrestle with it and talk about it and face it and cry about it, we would make quicker progress in healing and growing from it.

It's really an amazing story, but, honestly, I struggle with it. Was this a good thing that the angel did? I know one person each season was healed, but what was the fruit of the entire experience?

There was a packed pavilion hosting hurting, hopeless people. When the water stirred, it was a fend-for-yourself mad dash for the pool.

If you had lain for 38 years in impotency and each time you neared deliverance someone stepped on you and took your miracle, would that produce the fruit of the Spirit in you? Would you bless the man who tripped and elbowed you and sentenced you to another year of impotency?

This was a selfish environment, and the Scripture says that Jesus knew that this man had been there *"a long time."* He had spent a long time in an environment where everyone wanted to be first. There wasn't a servant's heart among them.

It was crowded. It was hot. People were impatient. They were mad. They were waiting for the slightest ripple. I wonder if there were some false starts.

I wonder if a sudden gust of wind ever troubled the water and signaled the start of the stampede. The race began, and someone got there first. This person flopped headfirst into the slimy sheep pool and stood up—still impotent and even more discouraged than ever. Their chance was blown. What would the odds be that they could get there first when it really counted?

This is the setting of our story. This is the setting of many Christian lives. Hurting, powerless, and waiting for something supernatural to fix everything, people lie in a selfish state of pain. Now, read the beginning of our text again. *"Jesus went up to Jerusalem."*

Into this place, Jesus comes.

Into this story, Jesus walks.

Into our lives, Jesus enters.

Into the sheep market, the Lamb of God comes.

Into the midst of impotency, walks omnipotence.

Into a slimy pool walks the source of living water.

Praise God! Aren't you glad Jesus didn't spend all His time hanging around the temple? I'm so glad He visits slimy pools and finds hurting people like me.

I like that the Scripture says He saw a "certain man." I always take special note when the Scripture uses the word "certain" because it's vague enough to apply to me. It could be any of us beside that pool.

A certain man had lain there for 38 years, and Jesus asked him in that place, *"Will you be made whole?"* Oh, my! This is a terrible question to ask an impotent man. He has no power! It's a slap in the face to ask such a question. The man was probably thinking, *Are you serious? If I had any power at all, I wouldn't be in this situation. If I had a choice in the matter, I wouldn't have spent the last 38 years lying in sheep dung.* I wonder why Jesus approached him this way.

I'm always very intrigued with the way Jesus interacted with people. Why would He move with compassion in one situation and then rebuke satan in the next? Sometimes He rebuked unbelief, and sometimes He asked, "Do you believe?" Sometimes He just healed, and sometimes He asked the person to do something like, "Show yourself to the priests, stretch out your hand, or wash in the pool." Why would Jesus say to a man with a 38-year-old weakness, "Are you going to be made whole?" Please note: Whatever this man's problem was, it had caused him to lie down. He had given up. The fight was long gone in him. Why, Jesus? I believe I can submit a possible answer.

I believe Jesus asked an impossible question to a desperate man because Jesus was fishing for another world-changer. This story occurs at the very beginning of Jesus' ministry. He was still in disciple-hunting mode, and Jesus saw *potential* in the *impotent* man. He saw the potential for greatness in a place of negativity and no power. Where this man couldn't do it, Jesus saw it done. How could Jesus see potential in this broken man? How could He see potential in a man who had lain there for 38 years? It's very simple. He saw potential in this man who had lain there for 38 years *because he had lain there for 38 years.* This man had hope! Jesus sees this same potential in you today!

What were the odds that he would ever be healed? He was so impotent that he was lying down. If he couldn't even stand, how could he ever get to the pool? He was incredibly discouraged, but he was still there. Some of you can relate to this man. You feel utterly defeated, but you're still here! That is victory.

Henry Dempsey is a modern-day example of this type of fortitude and determination.

On a commuter flight from Portland, Maine, to Boston, Henry Dempsey, the pilot, heard an unusual noise near the rear of the small aircraft. He turned the controls over to his co-pilot and went back to check it out.

As he reached the tail section, the plane hit an air pocket, and Dempsey was tossed against the rear door. He quickly discovered the source of the mysterious noise. The rear door had not been properly latched prior to takeoff, and it flew open. He was instantly sucked out of the jet.

The co-pilot, seeing the red light that indicated an open door, radioed the nearest airport, requesting permission to make an emergency landing. He reported that the pilot had fallen out of the plane, and he requested a helicopter search of that area of the ocean.

After the plane landed, they found Henry Dempsey— holding onto the outdoor ladder of the aircraft. Somehow he had caught the ladder, held on for ten minutes as the plane flew 200 mph at an altitude of 4,000 feet, and then, at landing, kept his head from hitting the runway, which was a mere twelve inches away. It took airport personnel several minutes to pry Dempsey's fingers from the ladder.[16]

A common analogy of the righteous in the Bible is the analogy of trees. Why is that? It's because a tree can go through a storm and emerge still standing. Oh, I know some of us have emerged from our nightmares leaning and bent, but we're still standing. Praise God for that! If you are reading this today, you're still here. You may be bent beyond recognition. You may feel that you've fallen and that your fall is fatal, but if you're here, you have potential—especially when the Lamb of God walks into the sheep market of your life.

Your 40's may be worse than your 30's, but your 30's will pale beside your 50's if you can answer the question correctly. Jesus says, "I'm fishing for world-changers today! Will you be made whole?" Will you? I believe you will.

It's here, at this place of questioning, that we hit the real problem of our story because our text tells us that *"the impotent man answered Him."* His problem was not the problem. The real problem was that the *impotent* man answered Him. He answered his potential with his impotency. Potential life stood before him, and he answered it with his impotency. Do we do the same?

He replied to Jesus, "Sir, I have no man." Oh, sometimes that's true, isn't it? We feel alone. We feel abandoned. Sometimes we *wait* alone. Grief can be incredibly lonely. Even when we have kind friends, they often can't relate to our situation so their genuine attempts to care can seem insensitive and shallow. At other times, our friends have no idea how to relate to us in our pain, so they quietly leave us. This happened to Jessica and me. In fact, it happened many times. Let's try our best to be gracious. Our friends are usually not cruel; they just aren't equipped. Neither are we.

"Sir, I have no man to put me into the pool." Sometimes people surround us, but they're just as impotent as we are. Sometimes we have people, but they just can't get us to the pool.

Have you ever tried to help someone? Have you ever thought, Oh, if they would only respond to this altar call…? Sometimes the moment comes, and the water is stirring, and you just can't get them there. I hate that feeling.

Although Jesus was very merciful and healed this man, He did it in spite of the man. This "certain" fellow didn't answer the question correctly. Instead of becoming a disciple, he called Jesus, "*Sir,*" and the Scripture says he *"knew not who [Jesus] was."* For me, I don't want to lie in defeat and hope that Jesus is merciful. I want to be proactive and stay in a position to receive wholeness. I want to answer the question correctly. Let me offer five keys that will help us answer this question.

Acknowledge the question.

Will you be made whole? The question contains a future verb tense. You're not whole now, and you must acknowledge your condition. It's okay to admit that you're living in a dazed state of disorientation. If all your theology makes perfect sense immediately after bereavement, you are probably in a bit of denial. God can handle your humanity. The man in our story wasn't even sure if Jesus was God, and yet he eventually testified before the entire pack of unbelieving religious leaders. You can be real. You *must* be real. Problems don't improve if left to themselves. For example, marriages do not positively evolve over the years. They require work and a consistent commitment to honestly face the issues.

You probably don't want to be real in every setting and with every person. The clerk in the grocery store may not really want to know the depths of your confusion and pain when she asks you how you're doing. The casual acquaintance at church may be a little alarmed if you unload both barrels in the foyer before service. However, most times do call for honesty.

If you can't be honest with your friends, find new friends. I don't mean that in a cold or critical way. I'm very serious. When Jessica and I walked through the dark night of our soul, we needed more mature friends who didn't feel the need to fix us or answer the tough questions. Sometimes all they did was cry. Sometimes that was the only appropriate response. You need friends like that. Acknowledge the question.

Acknowledge *who is asking the question.*

I said this is a terrible question (and it really is), until you acknowledge who is asking it. "*When Jesus saw him lie...He saith unto him, Wilt thou be made whole?*" (emphasis added). Who is asking the question? Jesus is! The Savior is posing the question to your hurting soul today. He wasn't just the Savior 2000 years ago; He's the Savior today. He wasn't just your Savior 1, 10, or 40 years ago when you were born again; He's your Savior right now. This isn't some stranger over a cash register; this is your Redeemer. This is the lover of your soul who has taken the time to count every hair on your head. This is Jesus. This is your Father. He loves you, and He isn't afraid of your answer. When you remember who is asking it, it will help you with the next step.

Acknowledge that you can answer **yes** *to the question.*

For some, the big hurdle will be admitting the problem and the need for healing, but for others, the challenge will be admitting that they *can* be healed. Your situation is not hopeless. Believe me, I am not writing these statements flippantly. This very week, I have spoken with a young woman who is terribly addicted to heroin and desires to be free, and I've spoken with a man who has had multiple affairs and is now trying to salvage his broken marriage. I know the deep pain of failure and loss. I know how hopeless it feels when someone from the outside says there is hope. Even so, I say, there is hope!

Do you remember where this story occurred? It occurred in Jerusalem. The impotent man thought, I *have experienced 38 years of failure. How could I ever be made whole? Jesus thought, I am standing in Jerusalem. In three short years, I will be crucified outside this very city. I will rip the keys of authority out of satan's hand, and I will rise from the dead and forever crush death, hell, and the grave—how can you not be made whole?*

We can answer "yes" because of He who asks the question.

Answer the question.

Once you evaluate the good, the bad, and the ugly, you still have to answer the question. If you don't answer it, you might not get the wholeness. What if this man had ignored Jesus? At least he called Jesus, "Sir." What if he had cursed Jesus and said, "Get out of my way. I'm waiting for the troubling of the water!" The Lord may have healed him out of pity, but He may have left and looked for someone like blind Bartimaeus. The Lord may heal you simply because He loves you, but the New Testament is clear that the majority of those who were healed cried out to the Son of David for mercy. I have no one, Lord—but I'll not miss the day of my visitation. I will be made whole! You don't have to feel whole to say "yes."

One of the great aspects of Christianity is that we can answer the question on behalf of someone else. What if you have a spouse or a family member or a loved one who is answering their potential with their impotency? What if Jesus speaks to them and they say, "I have no one Lord." I know I can't get anyone to the pool on my own, but I can approach the throne of grace and say, "Lord, since it's You who asks and empowers, I say on their behalf 'yes, they will be made whole.'"

Answer the question **with more than words.**

Jesus asked the question; He gave space to hear the answer; and then He said, "*Rise, take up your bed.*" Jesus used a very strong word when He said, "rise." The word *rise* means two things in the Greek language. First, it is a command for the dead to be raised. This is the divine element in our healing. The dead can do nothing to raise themselves. Second, it means to wake up and become attentive to one's dangerous position. This is our part of the bargain. We must have divine empowerment, but we must also do our part to respond. There are several ways that we can practically respond to His question. Let me conclude this chapter by mentioning two ways.

First, keep standing. Remember, you are a tree of righteousness. Winston Churchill said, "When you're going through hell, keep going." You may have gone through hell, but you didn't stop! You're still here. You're still standing. Oh, you may be lying down on the inside, feeling utterly defeated and forlorn; but do you remember that Isaiah tells us that even vigorous young men stumble badly (utterly fall)? Do you recall what he says they should do? Just wait. Do nothing but stand and wait for the Most High to revive you. The Lord commends you today for standing.

Second, worship. Sometimes we can be so busy praying for our deliverance that we have no time for our Deliverer. Jesus came to speak with the impotent man and initiate a relationship with him, but the man immediately began making excuses and explained his struggle. During our dark times, worship is often more appropriate than prayer. When we pray, we are often focused on our need. When we worship, we are focused on Him.

Prayer can be a great challenge for those who have experienced great tragedy. Tragedy seems to stand in opposition of the famous blessing Scriptures of the Bible, and prayer often confronts this paradox. I'm praying for a miracle, and a miracle is exactly what I didn't receive. How is that, Lord? The questioning can turn sour. I'm not advocating a blind ignoring of the paradox, but I am advocating tender times of worship from a position of surrender. Worship first, question second. This is the pattern Job established.

The Lord loves you, and the world needs you. Jesus asks today, "Will you be made whole?" He doesn't ask this question with His fingers crossed. He asks it knowing that He has the power to help you answer, "yes."

Will you be made whole? I know you will.

9

Pursue

Today is May 14, 2003. It's been exactly seven years since Alexis graced my world. This morning Jessica, Amber, Madelyn, and I wrote love notes to her and attached them to helium balloons that floated, hopefully, to Heaven. We hugged and kissed and cried and marveled how we could have lived so long without her. For a few moments, I felt such pain that I wondered if I have healed at all.

I know at some point we have to get back in the saddle. We are not destined to hurt for eternity, and we *will*, eventually, experience a desire to run again. I'm not quite as fast as I used to be. I don't enlist for new assignments with quite the same level of zeal I had in my youth, but I am ready to settle into the starting blocks again. Perhaps you feel that way too.

For those of us who have passionately pursued and come up short, there are some keys we should ponder before we set out in pursuit again. Pursuit is seldom inspiring. Sometimes it's downright excruciating. Despite the pain of pursuit, however, it is still possible to see the Lord perform exploits through our lives. In fact, King David had a comrade that lived this truth. I think I see him now…

꒳

Snowflakes settled softly on the forest floor carpeting the cold earth in a fresh blanket of purity. The air was still, allowing the gentle flakes to flutter, rather than fall, from the evening skies. A gentle hush permeated the forest as if any noise might shatter the pristine beauty of this wintry landscape. To an unhurried traveler, the snowy scene would appear beautiful—almost dazzling—in its brilliance. Almost.

On the forest floor amidst the trees, a fresh set of lion tracks was being buried by the snow. Watching the animal's trail disappear, the hunter cursed the snow as he quickened his pace along the tracks gliding as a noiseless phantom bent on pursuit.

He was Benaiah, a renegade warrior and comrade of David, the young shepherd, singer, giant-slayer exile whom he had met in the cave of Adullum. Benaiah was alone in the forest. Alone, except for the lion. He wiped a palm, sweaty despite the cold, gripped the hilt of his broadsword more firmly, squinted into the snow, and continued in hot pursuit.

Tracking the lion was easy. Its wide prints lay deep in the soft earth, and occasional flecks of blood still appeared along the trail despite the snow. Was this lion wounded, or was he stained in the blood of his latest victim? The question scarcely registered in Benaiah's thinking. All he knew was that he intended to go down and kill a lion in a pit on this snowy day.

He had overcome great odds before. Once, he slew two lion-like men from Moab. They were the true champions of their nation (some called them the lions of god), yet he had bested them with the skill and savagery of a desperate man. At another time, he slew an Egyptian giant. Armed with only a wooden staff, Benaiah had approached this better armed, seven-and-a-half foot tall warrior and crushed him to the ground. He plucked the spear from his hand and ran him through pinning him to the earth. A warrior since his childhood, Benaiah had fought as a mercenary, a bodyguard, a captain, and as a fugitive comrade of the future king of Israel. He had wrought great victories unscathed, and he had fallen wounded only to be spared death by the sovereign hand of God. Benaiah knew the battlefield. Tonight, however, the battle was different. There were no trumpets and no war cries. There were no reinforcements and no camaraderie of brothers born in adversity. He was alone. It was cold. The daylight was swiftly fading. His heavy garments impeded his movements…and he would wear a lion-skin garment by nightfall or never return from the forest.

﹌

First Chronicles 11:22 says, "*Benaiah…also had gone down and killed a lion in the midst of a pit on a snowy day.*" It's such a short verse of Scripture. We can read it so quickly that we miss the full weight of it. Tucked away as it is in the ledger of David's mighty men, it can almost get lost among the other accounts of daring exploits. Jashobeam slew 300 men at one time with only a spear. Eleazar routed an army in a barley field at Pasdammin, fighting until his hand stuck to his sword. Adino slew 800 at one time. Shammah defended his field against the Philistines until the Lord wrought a great victory. Benaiah simply went down. Yes, it was a snowy day, but does one lion compare to 800 men? Many hunters own lion-skin wall hangings. Was this truly an exploit worthy of Scripture's endorsement? I submit to you that Benaiah's advent in a snowy pit was the most heroic event of David's mighty men.

Not only did he face the worst possible foe in the worst possible place in the worst possible conditions, but he also established for us a blueprint of pursuit. How do we pursue? How do we pursue the new things of God? How do we pursue our enemies while reeling from the pain of personal tragedy and loss? Benaiah pursued while battling internal depression, grief, and despair; and he presents the model for us to follow.

He shows us that if we will *stay gathered, boldly face our enemy,* and *cling to Jesus,* we'll eventually be adorned in a lion-skin robe.

The Lion of Judah (the lover of our soul) will roar on our behalf, and He will clothe us in the hide of our enemy.

Before we examine the life of Benaiah, let me share a recent experience. In mid-January 2002, a guest speaker addressed our congregation in Colorado Springs, and at the outset of his message, he shared a simple word from the Lord for our church. He said, "Pursue the new in 2002." Pursue the new in 2002! What a great word it was. Inherent in the statement was two truths: First, there was something new for the people of God in 2002; but second, we had to pursue it. I scanned the crowd for their reactions, and I saw a myriad of response. Some cheered, ready to run headlong into the new. Others wept softly at the prospect of a new beginning. Still, others sat silent, their thoughtful expressions mirroring the state of my own soul. Pursue the new? It's hard to do. Especially when so many of God's dear children have passionately pursued, only to come up short of their dreams in the end. I realized that morning that in a given church setting, there were several different groups of people all hearing the same word: Pursue the new in 2002.

For the first group, this word could not have come any sooner. These zealous souls sat with their sights firmly set on the new that would soon be theirs in 2002. Already running in hot pursuit, this word ministered confirmation and encouragement to them as they ran.

I sensed that the second group consisted of sincere saints who genuinely loved the Lord, yet did not feel any great need to pursue. Happy and content, these experienced no compelling urgency to run hard after the new.

Sitting in that service, silently scanning the crowd and awash in memories from 1996, I found myself a member of yet another group. For us, when the command came to pursue, the thoughts arose:

Am I really up for another pursuit?

I know the price tag of pursuit.

I understand the cost of the chase.

Do I really have what it takes to run again?

No strangers to the race, these had indeed run fervently in the past without obtaining positive results. Hearts laden with hope-deferred sickness, these discouraged ones wondered if they had enough courage to pursue again.

I weighed the words carefully, realizing that when the prophet said them, they were anointed and inspiring. In the conference setting, amidst the sweet presence of God, I felt that I had already pursued and conquered and that the new was already mine. In fact, I could almost feel the neck of my enemy under my foot. The problem, however, was that I knew I couldn't live at that conference. The prophet wasn't moving home with Jessica and me. On Monday morning, the worship band would not be waiting in my living room ready to play sweet music that would usher me into the throne room of God. There would be no prophet waiting to encourage me as I poured my bowl of cereal. There would be no conference enthusiasm. There would only be life and the reality of pursuit.

Pursue the new. It's a wonderful word. However, in real life it never feels the way we think it will feel when the man of God says it—especially when we've pursued before and only experienced defeat. I pursued before, and I *didn't* recover all. Am I ready for another pursuit? Can I handle another defeat? Is that just my unbelief talking? Shouldn't I just trust God no matter what? Should I attend another conference?

It's easy to pursue for a little while. Anyone can sprint for 50 meters, but how do we pursue for a lifetime? How do we live in hot pursuit? Anyone can rise to a heroic level for a short time; but while heroes may surface during crisis, they are fashioned as they live life. It's easier to pull an all-nighter to seek God than it is to dutifully read the Bible and pray each morning. How do we live, in the real world, where we laugh and cry and win and lose, in hot pursuit? Remember, the question is not: How do we hotly pursue? I can do that. I can fast and pray and produce brilliant bursts of New Years' resolutions; but how do I live, faithfully, day by day, in hot pursuit of the promises of God?

Let's glean some insight as we watch Benaiah pursue.

When we first meet Benaiah in Scripture, he is a mercenary, and he is most likely one of the distraught souls who has joined themselves to David in the cave Adullum. Do you remember them? *"And everyone who was in distress, everyone who was in debt, and everyone who was discontented gathered to* [David]. *So he became captain over them"* (1 Sam. 22:2). Let me caution you as we continue: The truths revealed through Benaiah (and the other mighty men) are neither flippant nor trite. They are brutal. They are real. The mighty men of David were neither superheroes nor saints. They were real men. They were men who had been touched by loss, and consequently, they limped for a lifetime. When wounded, they bled and wanted to strike back. None of them dreamed of overthrowing a kingdom and rising to positions of prestige and honor. They just wanted to pay their creditors and live through another day. They were broken men who had had enough.

They were *distressed, in debt,* and *discontent.* Our English rendering of these Hebrew adjectives falls short of conveying the depth of the despair and disgrace inherent in their definitions. Our Bible tells us that when these mighty men of David, these men of renown, near mythical in the description of their valor, came to David in Adullum, they were in distress. Upon scanning this text, a Hebrew reader would conjure a very vivid mental picture of these distressed men, because the word *distressed* essentially means claustrophobia. It means to feel trapped and confined in a claustrophobic space. The circumstances of life had so pressed these warriors that they were suffocating. Their surrounding pressures had nearly crushed them into oblivion, and the only option left for them was to run. Attempting to flee the chokehold of their grief, they ran to David, who himself was another fleeing fugitive.

Distressed. Confined in a claustrophobic space. Oh, but isn't it interesting that a man who once felt he was suffocating in a narrow confine chose to go down into a claustrophobic little pit and kill a lion on a snowy day!

Well, not only were these men distressed, but they were also *in debt*. Again, referencing the Hebrew word definitions, it is clear to us that this does not merely mean that things were tight for them financially. The word implies such inability to repay creditors that the borrower attempts to escape by flight. They hadn't overcharged on some credit cards or bounced a few personal checks. They were wanted men. They were so devastated financially that they fled to the cave of Adullum. Undoubtedly, this financial ruin contributed to the choking, claustrophobia that drove them there.

Sadly, our verse contains another adjective. These men, including our hero, Benaiah, were also *discontented*. This is an interesting word, and its definition vastly differs from its English counterpart. To experience this kind of discontentment meant to experience six specific sensations.

First, it implies *bitterness*. Bitterness is the sign of an unhealed wound. When Benaiah came on the scene, he was a bitter man; and since we know bitterness always covers an injury, we know that he was a wounded man.

The problem with bitter individuals is that, while their wound is real, their bitterness becomes a defilement that deeply imbeds itself into their nature and taints their personalities, gifts, and ministries. Oh, dear friends, we must heal! Bitterness is evidence that we have failed to respond properly to hurt or loss or grief. I pray that these words do not seem cold or callous, but some wounds require reopening and cleansing. Some broken bones require resetting. Not even mighty men or women are immune.

Second, the word *discontented* means *sterility*. No power. No life. Not only were these distressed souls bitter, but they had no power to change.

Third, the word refers to the *heart crushing experience of family turmoil*. Family, more than any other agency or institution, can either bless or wound us deeply. The reason that pain from family turmoil pierces so swiftly is that nothing is dearer to our hearts as human beings than family. This was the Creator's sovereign design.

Families were made to reveal the glory of God to His creation. They were designed to be safe, nurturing, and equipping environments. No pain runs as deep as the betrayal of family or the death of family. Poll David's mighty men, and you would see that their hearts ached from divorce, abuse, rejection, and the death of sons and daughters. Many never recovered. The grief of family turmoil pressed them into claustrophobic confines that sentenced them to bitter living. Remember, these men were not God's enemies. In fact, Uriah the Hittite, one of David's faithful men who is listed in the genealogy of Jesus, was found there. These men can be found beside you in Sunday school and Bible college classes. These men can be you or me.

The fourth definition reveals another depressing glimpse into their pain. They were experiencing *grief from an unfulfilled death wish*. In other words, they were suicidal. Misfortune had so rocked their worlds that upon awakening each morning, they grieved the thought of another day. Please hear me, these men were not unstable weaklings. Let me remind you that Job himself cursed the day of his birth. Elijah fell so low as to invoke death. Even Jonah, after successfully completing God's mission, asked the Lord if he might die. I have been this low. I have grappled with despair, and I've done it often.

I thank the Lord for what I heard Francis Frangipane say about the nature of the Lord. He said that the Lord's nature is like water—that it always goes to the deep places first. Oh, praise God! He isn't afraid of the dark night of our soul. He's not offended when we are afraid of the night. In fact, Scripture says that He is often found in thick darkness.

The fifth and sixth descriptions, respectively, are *personal hardship and disillusionment.*

When Benaiah first ducked his head inside the cave of Adullum, he was a shattered man. Emotionally and spiritually claustrophobic and fleeing creditors as he teetered on the edge of bankruptcy, he resembled no great warrior. He was bitter, sterile, and suicidal from great familial trauma. On top of all this, when we first meet him he is a mercenary—a feared and despised scoundrel.

Distressed. In debt. Discontent. Claustrophobic. Financially ruined. Bitter. Sterile. Heartbroken from family turmoil and tragedy. Depressed unto suicide. Disillusioned and floundering.

Our mighty men of David, including Benaiah, were marked by all of these. What did they learn that enabled them to heal? How were they able to rebuild? Embittered men could never install true kingly authority to a nation and protect the messianic line. How did they recover? How in the world does a guy like Benaiah pursue? How did David pursue?

I'm sure David felt like Benaiah when his family was lost at Ziklag, his city was razed, and his loyal men spoke of stoning him. To David, in that place, this word of the Lord came, "Pursue, for you shall surely overtake them and without fail, recover all." To Benaiah in Adullum the word came—"pursue." When I was Benaiah in a hospital room in Spokane, the word came to me as well—"pursue." To you, dear reader, in your tragic, grief-ridden state, the word repeats—"pursue."

Commodore McDonough pursued amidst pain and against great odds.

After McDonough's great victory over the British fleet on Lake Champlain, the commander of the British land forces, Sir George Provost, sent to him to inquire the secret of his success. He replied, writing on the sheet which contained the inquiry, "Hard fighting." He pursued on the battle, though his ship, the Saratoga, was riddled with shot, twice on fire, and in a sinking condition. He was twice knocked down, and reported killed, but revived and returned to the gun, which he sighted till victory was gained.[17]

Back to Benaiah. From all natural perspectives, fortune had not smiled upon him. He had a father, however, whose name was Jehoiada. First Chronicles 11:22 says, *"Benaiah was the son of Jehoiada."* *Jehoiada* means Jehovah knows. Remember with me that in the Hebrew culture a person's name denoted their character. Benaiah's father was Jehoiada, and he was characterized by the knowledge of God. In that wisdom, that only Jehovah knows, he made a very wise decision. He chose to raise his precious son Benaiah in a little town called Kabzeel. The name *Kabzeel* means whom Jehovah has gathered. It must have been a community of men and women whom God had assembled. Whom Jehovah has gathered! Wow! I'd like to raise my children there and faithfully love my wife there!

Jehoiada, a valiant man of God, must have lived so near the heart of God that his very nature spoke of the wisdom and understanding of God. In this heavenly understanding, he thought, *I want to raise my family among those whom God has gathered.* How does a man like Benaiah pursue? How do people like you and I pursue? I believe the first step of our pursuit is to stay gathered.

Does this sound too insignificant to warrant mention? Does this go without saying? I don't think so. I've watched many loyal saints wander off during times of crisis. It is not human nature to reach out when wounded. Our first response to pain is to recoil and retreat. Jessica and I have waved good-bye through tears to many friends and loved ones who left amidst this process. Let Him gather you into a family and then stay there.

Of course, there are no perfect families, and there are no perfect church families. When we're hurting and vulnerable, the imperfections and insensitivities in others stand out in bold font. We *will* be hurt by those closest to us, but they do love us. Most people just haven't been taught how to befriend those who are hurting. (I'll cover this at length in a later chapter.) But we still need to stay where He's set us.

Benaiah understood the value of assembly. He was eventually able to stand alone in a snowy pit because he had made it a practice to stand arm in arm with the brethren. It reminds me of the instructions given to the weeping women at the empty tomb of Jesus. The angel said to them, "*Why do you seek the living among the dead? He is not here, but is risen!...But go, tell His disciples...* (see Lk. 24:5; Mk. 16:6-7)." Essentially, he said, "Stay gathered! Life is about to visit the brethren!"

Jehoiada knew the trials of the living. He understood that the earthly inheritance of the redeemed was not merely peace, blessing, and prosperity, but also trauma, grief, and paradox. So he moved to Kabzeel where God was gathering and establishing, and here, in this place, baby Benaiah was born.

We must stay gathered.

Jehoiada did this, and his labor was reflected in the name of his son, for *Benaiah* means whom Jehovah has built. Oh, how exciting this sounds to be built by Jehovah Himself. What an honor! What a sacred separation from the common place. Oh, to be built by Jehovah! What a delight for parents to know that God Himself is building a work within their children. I can think of no greater gift than to know that Jehovah has built a strong foundation and strong walls of protection within my daughters. Truly, this is the heart cry of every godly parent. We must remember, however, that if God desires to build *on* our life, He must first build *in* it, and that building process can be excruciating. It almost killed David. It almost killed Benaiah. It almost killed me.

When we hear the word "build," we automatically think of building *up*. We think of the creation of something that wasn't there. We must remember, if we desire to be built by Jehovah, the building process begins *down*. Once plans are assembled and a vision is established for a new building structure, a foundation must be dug. Hard places of earth must be softened, and rocks must be removed. Beloved, you know as well as I that the bigger a building is to be, the deeper its foundation must be. You can throw up a storage shed overnight, but a cathedral requires years of work. The bigger the Lord desires to build us, the deeper He must excavate in us. This excavation can be agonizing.

The Lord wanted to build some great things in Benaiah. In fact, Benaiah would become an indispensable factor in the success of King David and the propagation of his reign. Benaiah's career was marked by unswerving loyalty to David and, eventually, Solomon as well. Read with me the resumé of this great man.

During his pre-king days, David had *three* and *thirty* honorable, mighty men, and Benaiah is mentioned in each group.

Benaiah became the head of David's personal bodyguards.

He became the head of a 24,000-man division who regularly served the king.

He succeeded Joab as commander of the entire army.

He was a key factor in the power struggle between Solomon and Adonijah (Solomon's treacherous older brother who sought to steal the throne). On the heels of Benaiah's service in this matter, First Kings 2:46 tells us, *"The kingdom was established in the hand of Solomon."*

Yes, Benaiah had a great destiny, and the Lord built a strong tower in his life; but we know that his building and preparation experience was excruciating, because when we first met him, he had a death wish. When Benaiah came on the scene in the cave of Adullum, he was broken, desperate, heartsick, sterile, and disillusioned. How did such a man become the greatest of David's mighty warriors? I personally believe that the turning point occurred on a snowy day when he also "had gone down and killed a lion in the midst of a pit." Benaiah went down, and he faced the worst foe in the worst place in the worst conditions. He knew what he was after. He didn't stumble upon a lion's lair while hunting elk. Benaiah went down. He chose to go down. Alone. He didn't take an army. Are you willing to go down? Am I? Once the lion roars, there is an adrenaline rush to sustain us; but to take the first step down, now that requires character. It's easy to vow pursuit when we are in the camp with our brothers in arms; but to take the first step down alone? How terrifying.

Benaiah went down...and discovered that pursuit is seldom inspiring. Oh, it's an inspiring story. It's an inspiring verse—in fact, it's a preaching verse! The heartbroken man had had enough. He's the Lone Ranger and the Terminator rolled into one. This guy sounds unstoppable. In all honesty, however, I sure wouldn't feel like crawling into a pit with a lion on a snowy day. On snowy days, I like to wear my pajamas and drink hot chocolate. If I'm feeling truly daring, I might shovel the front walk. But to climb into a pit? To face a lion? Intentionally?! I think the Lazy Boy would sound quite appealing at that moment in time. Like it or not, the Lord has targeted some lions for extinction, and he's destined you and me to annihilate them.

We must boldly face our enemy.

Spiritual warfare is a reality. We *will* fight, and we will fight often. Some battles occur simply because we are Christians, but others are absolutely pivotal for the advancement of our callings. Some battles are launching pads to the throne of our destinies. First Chronicles 11:22 said he *"also* had gone down." *Also*—in addition to his other exploits—he faced the lion. He had to. "Benaiah, it's not enough that you have faced *lion-like men* of Moab, you have to also face the lion itself. Only one of you will emerge, but this is the doorway to your destiny. Benaiah, are you willing to go down?"

*"Benaiah had gone **down**."* We don't go up for these types of struggles. Although we're gathered, and we love the Body of Christ, there are times when no one can swing your sword but you. *You* must pursue. This is a very troubling thought in light of the nature of your foe. *"He also had gone down and killed a **lion**."* This wasn't a lynx or a cougar or some renegade Philistine; this was the king of beasts. You don't just stroll into close quarters and take its crown.

It's one thing to bait a lion and shoot it from a distance. It's quite another to pay it an unexpected visit in its lair. It's one thing to stand on a hill and swing your battle-ax at a downward stroke toward your foe, but when the command to "pursue" takes you *into* a pit, things are quite different. There is no room to run in a pit. There's not even room to duck and dodge. There is only room to kill or be killed.

This type of warfare is especially perplexing, because not only was Benaiah hurting, weary, distressed, and about to jump into a lion's pit, but he was doing it on a *snowy* day. Snowy days decrease our visibility, and sometimes we have to fight even when the vision isn't clear. He was pursuing—even when questions existed about the particulars of the vision. The word of the Lord was "pursue." The details may have been fuzzy, but the chase had to go on.

Another simple aspect to winter battles is that wintry days are cold. Cold days require heavier garments that can impede movement. Also, joints are stiffer in the winter season of life. Old wounds begin aching again. My wife understands this. She suffered a fall during a choreographed dance in 1993 that crushed her ACL. (I don't need to tell you that it was *my* clumsy lift and throw that precipitated the injury.) After hours of prayer and three surgeries, the doctors say that her injured knee is stronger that her other one. Even so, on cold days, there is a stiffness that seems to permeate the joint. You and I can be truly healed, but winter battles can cause old wounds to ache again. They can throb and threaten to reopen. The simple rapping of the knuckles can feel like a mortal wound on a frostbitten day.

There have been times in my Christian walk when it seemed I was Tarzan. Wearing only a loincloth, free to hurtle through the treetops, I could tackle anything. I, not some skulking lion, was king of the jungle and I could run, jump, climb, and wrestle with the best of them. I've always loved the Word of the Lord! How could I ever end up wearing a snowsuit over my armor, barely able to stand in a cramped, slippery pit on a gloomy, hot chocolate-and-pajamas type of day?

On slippery footing, with increased vulnerability, weary warriors must be very careful. We must cling to the Great Physician and trust that His work in our life has not been in vain. Ask Him, "Am I still wounded, or is this just a winter day?" Cling to Him in the pit, because when we are cold and stiff and weary and looking very much like a target to our enemy, we are more prone to the wounding that leads to offense. Please, hear this advice: When you are in this state where the Word of the Lord can appear to be a mockery, make no sudden moves—except to hurl yourself at your enemy! There's really no alternative. With the lion's steamy breath just inches away, all we can do is charge. Remember that Jesus didn't send you down there to feed one of His lions. He wants to clothe you in a lion-skin robe.

The March 1988 *Rotarian* tells the story of a certain organization offering a bounty of $5,000 for wolves captured alive. It turned Sam and Jed into fortune hunters. Day and night they scoured the mountains and forests looking for their valuable prey.

Exhausted one night, they fell asleep dreaming of their potential fortune. Suddenly, Sam awoke to see that they were surrounded by about fifty wolves with flaming eyes and bared teeth. He nudged his friend and said, "Jed, wake up. We're rich!"[18]

I'm confident that you are wearing a lion's pelt for a jacket today. I'm sure you look good in it! In many areas of your life, the Lord has probably been able to mold you into a worthy warrior. However, there may be an area of your Christian walk that seems to have slipped into winter. Night may have fallen over an area of your life, or your family, or your friendships. In fact, you may feel the snowflakes settling softly over you right now.

It was probably a beautiful day when Benaiah woke up and saw snow. It may have even felt cuddly and cozy—except that there was a wild carnivore that needed slaying and a word from the Lord that said, "pursue."

Despite the fear. Despite the darkness. Despite the cold, foreboding pit, I have good news for you. God has gathered you! He's building something wonderful into your life! If you can stand in your slippery, snowy day, you'll stand in king's palaces.

Benaiah's story is not quite over. When the screaming and the snarling and the clawing and the cursing were over, he alone emerged from that snowy pit. He went down a heartbroken man—suicidal even. He came up victorious, leaving a bloody carcass in a would-be grave, and that particular lion would never again walk around seeking whom it might devour.

Benaiah never should have survived. He should have been a dead man. My faith should have never survived our pursuit of

Alexis' healing. My confidence in a healing, loving, all-powerful God should have never survived the staggering loss and pain we experienced through her death. Mine was not the faith of Daniel in the lion's den. Mine was the trembling, fearful, slippery stance of one in whom Jehovah was trying to build.

How did Benaiah survive? How did I survive? Why do I still love Him and glory in His plan for mankind? Am I a mighty man of faith? Certainly not! Have I reconciled my grief and my questions? Actually, I carry more. How do lion-slayers survive? *They survive because Jesus went down first!*

We must cling to Jesus.

To survive this word of the Lord, the giver of the word must join you in the pit!

The Lion of Judah also went down and slew a devil that likes to masquerade as a lion, in a pit on a snowy day. Do you think it may have been a cold day in hell when Jesus showed up there? I imagine that hell froze over when satan thought he had truly crucified the Savior of the world only to see Him show up in his own lair. In fact, they probably did a little figure skating on the lake of fire, when the Lion of Judah showed up in hell to strip the keys from satan and take captivity captive.

Jesus goes down first. Cling to Him. He doesn't have all the answers—He is the answer. Even if vision is dim and footing is uncertain, the Lion of Judah will eventually roar on your behalf. The lover of your soul will clothe you in the hide of your enemy if you stay the course. You'll find that not one tear was wasted. Not one prayer was snuffed out before the throne. He is for you.

Pursue, for you shall surely overtake them and without fail, recover all!

10

Anchor My Soul

"Someone has to go first!"

"Voices don't cry where everything has been settled!"

"The only highways to the future are the ones we build!"

"Somebody's got to fight the devils!"

"God's assignments are always God-sized!"

"Spiritual pioneers must be able to open a hard heaven, and they must be able to go several days without a drink of water!"

It was a young adult leadership conference in 1999, and my pastor was on a roll. What a message! I think every person in the room that evening enlisted to serve as spiritual pioneers. I know I did. I didn't do it with a lot of hype and enthusiasm, however, because this particular message was preached within weeks of Alexis' third birthday, and Jessica and I were tired. It probably sounded exciting to be a spiritual pioneer, but we felt as if we were human pincushions pierced with the arrows of the natives. The life of a settler was looking more attractive all the time.

It was only May, and Alexis had already been hospitalized several times that year with pneumonia. With each hospitalization came the inevitable question, "Are you ready to let her go?" Of course we weren't! She wasn't supposed to live a year, and she had already tripled her life expectancy. Surely the Lord would perform a miraculous healing for her.

She had become my hero many months earlier. There is no possible way she could have been any sweeter. She carried the peace and presence of God in a profound way. Home health care nurses who cared for her felt compelled to study the Bible and recommit their lives to the Lord. Hospital nurses graciously fought over who would be allowed to watch her in her frequent hospitalizations. When she went to Heaven, two pediatric specialists, one family doctor, and eight nurses attended her memorial service. She touched many lives. She certainly touched mine. At three years old, she had endured more than any human's share of suffering.

When this message came to us about being spiritual pioneers, my faith wasn't wavering, but my emotions were. I still believed God, but I was about to slip off the end of my rope. Let me share an excerpt from my journal that I recorded one week prior to this leadership conference and its appeal for pioneers.

> *For three years now I've had a promise from God, and I've only seen the opposite occur. I have experienced every possible range of emotion. I've moved from faith to despair and from hate to love. I'm lucky and grateful to still be here. I'm so very tired, but I know that I could testify all night of what the Lord has done in my life during this season. One primary thing has emerged in me: Having seen how fragile life is, having become an eyewitness of the hurting people that fill our hospitals daily, having gone through my own heart-wrenching experiences, I have become consumed with a passion to make my life count for the Kingdom of God. I don't want to be average and survive my time on planet Earth and someday slip through the pearly gates of Heaven. I want to fulfill every nuance of my destiny!*

Today, over four years later, I still feel that way. I feel about 40 years older. I feel a little uglier and a little slower to enlist for pioneering assignments, but with every bit of my being, I still want to impact my world for Jesus. I want to make Alexis proud. I want the cloud of witnesses to call her away from the feet of Jesus to watch me fight and pray and believe and love and faithfully follow my calling. You probably feel that way too.

I'm sure you don't want your pain to be wasted. I'm sure you want the Lord to use your suffering for His glory. How does that happen? There's no inherent glory in the suffering. Just enduring trials doesn't bring Him honor. The Lord is glorified when the devil plays his last card with us, and we're still in the game. He's honored when we can say, "I've seen enough to make me an infidel, but I'm still a lover of His presence." I love the Scripture in First Kings 5:1 (KJV) that says that King Hiram was *"ever a lover of David."* I want that to be me! I want to *ever be a lover of Jesus.* I also love Psalm 84:4 that says of the righteous, *"They will still be praising You."* If someone checks on me later in life and asks, "Whatever happened to him? Where is he after all these years?" I want the swift reply to come, "Oh, he's still praising! You can find him in the sanctuary. He still loves Jesus. He still aspires to serve Him."

The Lord wants to take you to a new place, but if it's a new place, it means there is no road. Someone needs to blaze a trail for others to follow. Psalm 125 is a trailblazing psalm, and its first two verses shed some light on how to survive our trial and blaze our trail:

> *Those who trust in the Lord are like Mount Zion, which cannot be moved, but abides forever. As the mountains surround Jerusalem, so the Lord surrounds His people from this time forth and forever.*

These wonderful words introduce one of the songs of ascents or songs of degrees. There are several of these songs in the Book of Psalms. They were known as pilgrim songs. They were songs sung by traveling, worshipping pilgrims on their way to Jerusalem to offer sacrifices to the Lord. They were called songs of ascent because Jerusalem was perched on the top of a very high mountain at the end of a very long, winding road.

These worshippers had to climb and circle, and climb and circle. They would worship and climb and pant from their exertions; and after they felt they could climb no further, they would suddenly round a corner and see Jerusalem. It was in a setting like this, crowded by throngs of worshippers from all over Israel, that Psalm 125 occurred. These singing mountain climbers were spiritual pioneers. They were men and women who so desired God's presence that they journeyed to find it. These pilgrims were a lot like us.

I heard an old preacher once say, "The average Christian is more like a struggling pilgrim than an overcoming conqueror." That quote may not go over very well at a young adult leadership conference, but it's worth considering. It's true that all the promises of God are yes and amen in Jesus, but it's equally true that our primary citizenship is not of this world. We who are born again are citizens of Heaven, and our earthly pilgrimage is short. We cannot be shortsighted, and judge God, based only on what happens in our brief lives on earth. Paul said, *"If in this life only we have hope in Christ, we are of all men most miserable"* (1 Cor. 15:19 KJV). We cannot recover fully from grief with only an earthly perspective. Let's get to Heaven and then, with His bird's-eye view, make our judgments. One of the primary ways to access a heavenly perspective while still on earth is to worship.

The power of worship cannot be overstated. It is healing balm for a broken soul. In his book, *Tell Your Heart To Beat Again*, Dutch Sheets says this about the power of praise and worship:

> One of the ways we draw near is through praise and worship. I know it sounds terribly simplistic—and I would never make light of your pain—but I believe that any person's life could be radically and forever changed by extreme doses of praise and worship. Simply applying worship in the same way that one

would therapy—taking an hour or two each day and declaring the greatness of God—would create a place for the Lord to set up His throne in our hearts (see Ps. 22:3). From there He would be able to rule over the areas of hurt.[19]

If you're still reading this book, it's safe for me to assume that your pilgrimage has taken you on an uphill climb. You've been climbing and climbing and spiraling and getting dizzy, and you're very possibly out of breath. Often it's difficult to sing and worship during our pilgrimage because we're climbing this long, winding hill, and we lose our breath. Remember, the Hebrew and Greek words for *spirit* (including the Holy Spirit) contain in their definitions the word *breath*. Sometimes we get out of spirit on our journey. We run out of the anointing. We need a new anointing to sustain us in our pilgrimage.

This particular pilgrim learned an extremely crucial lesson at this point in his journey. If we would make it to the top of our mountain, we must learn it too. If we can learn what he learned, we'll finish strong. At the end of this pilgrim's journey, he knew that *God surrounded him.* We know he made it to Jerusalem because of the second verse, "*As the mountains surround Jerusalem, so the Lord surrounds His people.*" He saw those beautiful mountains surrounding Jerusalem, and he was overcome with a sense of awe as he received the revelation that God Himself surrounded him with the same strength and majesty. He saw a picture of security and confidence in the Lord.

I want to tell you today that the Lord surrounds your life! As the glorious mountains surround the holy city of Jerusalem, so He surrounds you forever. The mountains stand strong even if you don't believe they're there. I have a view of Pike's Peak from my bedroom window, and if I wake up in the morning and don't believe in mountains, it will still confront my gaze. Remember, this pilgrim was low on the Holy Spirit. Even when he was out of breath and couldn't sing, the mountains were still there.

Our pilgrim learned this, and he learned something else too. He learned (according to verse 3) that the scepter of the wicked would not remain over the lot of the righteous. He learned that even if the enemy seems entrenched on the land, he will not remain so forever. At the end of his journey, he learned that the power of the enemy would eventually break, and that good would be accomplished.

It's a positive thing to reflect on what you have experienced and evaluate how it has marked your life for the good. Often, the incidents that have hurt you the most have also produced the very essence of your life message. Preach it! Dr. Sam Sasser once said that prophets must sob out the message in their own lives first. Through the painful trials of life, we become marked with His heart in a special way, and we receive a message. Every survivor, every spiritual pioneer, has a special message to carry to their generation. You have faced specific trials and tragedies that I have never been asked to endure. Those crucibles have produced revelation in you that I do not possess.

Out of our brokenness and pain, God knows how to bring healing and life. It's true that the healed can become the healers.

Dutch Sheets related a story that shows how beauty can shine from the midst of brokenness.

> At the Royal Palace of Tehran, in Iran, you can see one of the most beautiful mosaic works in the world. The ceilings and walls flash like diamonds in multifaceted reflections.

> Originally, when the palace was designed, the architect specified huge sheets of mirrors on the walls. When the first shipment arrived from Paris, they found to their horror that the mirrors were shattered. The contractor threw them in the trash and brought the sad news to the architect.

Amazingly, the architect ordered all of the broken pieces collected, then smashed them into tiny pieces and glued them to the walls to become a mosaic of silvery, shimmering, mirrored bits of glass.

Broken to become beautiful! It's possible to turn your scars into stars. It's possible to be better because of the brokenness. It is extremely rare to find in the great museums of the world objects of antiquity that are unbroken. Indeed some of the most precious pieces in the world are only fragments that remain a hallowed reminder of a glorious past.[20]

We need to hear from people who have endured their crucibles and still crossed the finish line strong. I can encourage you, but I'm still in the race; and I have a lot of life left to run. It's nice to hear from older, seasoned saints who have proven themselves faithful and have found the Lord to be faithful as well. As an old man, David wrote in Psalm 37:25, *"I have been young, and now am old; yet I have not seen the righteous forsaken, nor his descendants begging bread."* He couldn't have written that as a young man. I'm still a young man, and I have felt forsaken plenty of times. I wonder what I'll say when I'm an old man. I'll probably say, "Your battle will come to an end. The stronghold that is hindering you will eventually break in Jesus' name."

There is a footnote added in verse three that we would be wise to heed. We must be very careful in this pre-breakthrough season of life. The rest of verse three tells us that when the scepter of the enemy remains on the promised land for an extended period of time, the righteous are tempted to use their hands for evil. The word *evil* means to distort or twist. Please hear this point: When we are hoping for a breakthrough or a miracle and it hasn't happened yet, we can be tempted to adopt a distorted view of God.

Based on this psalm, it seems that this pilgrim was tempted to use his hands for evil. Songs of ascents were written in the stark reality of life, and he couldn't have written about these things unless he had experienced them. He must have experienced an enemy scepter over his promise; he must have been tempted to do evil; and he must have seen the enemy's scepter shatter. Remember, the mountains still surround you, whether you can see them or not. Even if the mountains are fogged in and invisible to your eyes, you are still surrounded. He still loves you, and your story is not over yet.

"Those who trust in the Lord are like Mount Zion, which cannot be moved, but abides forever" (Ps. 125:1). If you're going to make it forever, it will be because you've *abided* forever. Some translations use the word *endure* instead of abide. It takes spiritual guts to endure. If you let go of your dreams easily, you'll never accomplish anything great for God. How do we endure? In what should we abide? Are we to grit our teeth and tough it out? The definition of this word contains three powerful keys that will help us. These keys are the primary principles for abiding.

The word *abide* means: "attach oneself to, confide in, and feel secure." Notice the sequence. Attach...confide in...feel secure. I have found that my level of security directly equals my level of confiding and abiding.

Attach to. Have you ever heard of the postage stamp anointing? It's the ability to stick to something until you get there. Professional rock climbers use special resistance machines designed specifically to strengthen their fingertips. Find your place and cling to it even if it's only by your fingertips. Sometimes we must tighten our seat belt and ride out the storm. Yes, the Lord is our comforter and helper, but we must make a determined effort to get to Jerusalem. We've got an appointment with the King, and we aren't going to miss it.

Confide in. A major key in abiding is confiding. Is the Lord your confidante? Do you tell Him everything? Do you express to Him your every emotion from outrage to contentment? You can trust Him. He's God enough for your problem, and He's compassionate enough for your humanity.

Feel secure. When we are firmly attached and fully confiding, we begin to feel secure. It's a very natural progression. How can you ever feel secure if you aren't closely attached? How can you feel safe if you haven't honestly confided and then received acceptance? By the way, you become secure (firmly held) in whatever you attach to and confide in.

If you attach to Jesus, you'll be as secure as our pilgrim. You'll be as secure as Jerusalem snuggled within a mighty mountain range. However, this principle doesn't apply only to Jesus. *Your security stems from your attachment.* If you attach to a lie, you will become secure in a lie! Words go deep. I heard Francis Frangipane say words are like molten steel that enter a young person and shape their character and identity. Some people are secure in their insecurity. Some people have rock-solid security in the belief that they are only second-rate people. To who or what are you attached? You'll become secure there.

What are some things we can attach ourselves to that will produce an unshakable security in our lives? In what can we abide that will yield stability and healing? How about First Corinthians 13:13? This familiar Scripture says, *"And now abide faith, hope, love, these three; but the greatest of these is love"* (emphasis added). Let's focus here for a moment.

Since the greatest abiding force is love, our priority should be to abide in love. One way we can abide in love is to practice the principle of sowing and reaping with our love. To receive love, love. Sow love. First John 4:18 says *"Perfect love casts out fear."* I used to view this verse as simply meaning that the perfect love of God drives out my fear, and while that is true, I've come to believe there's more to it than that. His love does drive out my fear, but my love, when it is perfect, also drives out fear. *Perfect* means full-grown, adult as opposed to infancy. When I practice and share selfless, mature, full-grown love it has a healing effect in my own soul.

In addition to practicing selfless love, we can also learn to abide in love by responding to His love for us. First John 4:19 says *"We love Him because He first loved us."* I realized once that this Scripture doesn't apply merely to our initial salvation experience. It refers to the principle that *He is always loving us.* Every time your heart is stirred and you whisper in reverence, "Lord, I love You," He has already been loving you first. The more correct statement on our part is "Lord, I love You, too."

It can be difficult to abide in love. Jude said to *"Keep yourselves in the love of God"* (Jude 21). The world, the devil, and your own fears will try to sway you from the revelation that He has been, is, and forever will be, in love with you. Attach to His love.

The other areas of attachment for us in First Corinthians 13 are faith and hope. Faith is the assurance that the word from the Lord will happen. Faith truly sees the end. It moves mountains, and it releases the will of God in earth. Most of us have this kind of faith in certain areas. We've seen mountain ranges move in particular areas of our life. However, there are also areas of our life where we lack faith. This lack of faith should not induce condemnation because the first step to building faith is easy: Begin to hope.

As Rubem Alves once said, "Hope is hearing the melody of the future. Faith is to dance to it."[21]

Hope is beautiful, and it always comes before faith. Faith is the assurance of things hoped for. If there is no hope, there is no assurance. If you are trying to build faith without first building hope, you will fail. We must begin with hope.

I'm sure this word inches me out onto thin ice, because I know your hopes have probably been dashed in areas. So have mine. I realize that it's dangerous to talk about hope after devastation and destruction because to hope again is to risk disappointment again.

If we break the word *disappointment* down, we see an *appointment* with a negative (*dis*) stuck to it. Sometimes our appointments with miracle power have been put off for so long that we can get fearful and cynical. Our hopes have been repeatedly dashed after being raised in expectation, and now disappointment permeates our being. It's a tough position to be in, and we run the risk of offense and bitterness taking root in our souls.

Romans 5:5 says, "*Hope does not disappoint.*" How can this be? I would never have experienced disappointment had I not hoped. Had I never hoped for a miracle for my baby, I would only be facing grief and pain right now, instead of grief and pain plus confusion, shaken theology, and hope-deferred heartsickness (see Prov. 13:12).

What is hope? The New Testament word *hope* is the Greek word *elpis*. *Elpis* is the desire for good with *some* expectation of receiving it. It's not quite faith, but it's more than a wish. It's not the absolute assurance, but it is desire mixed with *some* expectancy. Hebrews 10:23 says to "*Hold fast the profession of our faith without wavering*" (KJV). The word translated "faith" in this text is actually the Greek word *elpis*. The Lord doesn't expect rock-solid faith, but He does expect us to hope. Hope is something we can do. Faith brings the answer, but sustained hope brings faith. Faith only comes by hearing, but hope positions us to hear the Word.

Zechariah 9:12 is an interesting Old Testament passage that contains the phrase, "*Return to the stronghold, you prisoners of hope.*" I like that…*prisoners of hope*. The Hebrew word for "hope" is *awesome*. Its root definitions are as follows:

1. To attach (as with a cord).

2. To bind together.

3. The opening of a dungeon.

4. Jail-delivery.

5. To open (this last definition is the most basic root meaning of the word).

Hope opens! When we bind ourselves to hope, jail cells open. There is a critical point to be made here. We can't just passively hope. We must bind ourselves to it. We must commit for a lifetime to keep hoping. Hebrews 6 says that hope contains enough power to open up the veil to the holy of holies (where Jesus went before us) and secure an anchor for our soul. Hope takes us to a place of intimacy with the Lord that we can find nowhere else. To be hurting, broken, and disappointed and still say, "Nevertheless I still hope in your Word" is to release a power that is life-changing and life-producing. It will take us out of our circumstance and lead us inside the veil. Here, inside the holy of holies, anchored with Jesus, our faith will begin to grow.

Here's the problem: This is a process. We usually don't receive a promise today, anchor our soul in hope to it tomorrow, and have a miracle by the weekend. It often takes time, and satan attacks us with discouragement in the middle of the process. Proverbs 13:12 says, *"Hope deferred makes the heart sick."* The nature of hope is to expect, but when hope is deferred long enough, we develop heartsickness. Another way of saying it is this: Heartsickness occurs after constant disappointment. We thought we had an appointment with the promise, but it didn't come to pass. Out of our disappointment, we became heartsick and stopped setting appointments. We stopped hoping, and consequently, we became critical and cynical; and these never enter through the veil. If we don't do something at this point, our quest for destiny will end here.

Be encouraged—the power of hope does not die easily. Romans 5:5 says, *"Hope does not disappoint, **because the love of God has been poured out in our hearts...**"* (emphasis added). Hope sets us up for disappointment, but hope does not disappoint.

In *Tell Your Heart To Beat Again*, Dutch addresses those battling with hope-deferred heartsickness:

And there is music left in you! I know you can play hope's song, even in the dark night of the soul. There is hope in the night; and there is music somewhere in your soul. Don't give up.[22]

The power of hope is often underestimated. There are five power points of hope.

1. **Everyone can hope.** You may not have rock-solid faith, but you are able to hope. No one starts with perfect faith. They start with hope.

2. **Hope lifts us above the present circumstances.** Hope can lift a prisoner out of his cell.

3. **Hope can flourish during oppression.** Chains cannot quench the power of hope. No one and nothing can take our hope unless we surrender it.

4. **Hope does not disappoint** (we'll expound this in just a moment).

5. **Hope anchors us to the lover of our soul.**

Look at another Old Testament picture of hope's power. Hosea 2:14-18 is a tremendous picture of the Lord, who first loved us, leading us into the wilderness (like spiritual pioneers). He allures us and speaks to us *tenderly* (the word literally means to have a heart-to-heart conversation). Here, in this place, He gives us the valley of *Achor* (meaning "trouble") as a door of hope. When hope opens a door in the midst of our trouble, we suddenly see a vineyard (new wine/anointing) where a parched desert once stood. We experience restoration while a youthful song fills our weary soul and breathes fresh spirit (breath) into us. We sing as in the days of our youth as we ascend with Him (no longer merely our Lord, but now our husband).

The end result of sustained hope is faith. Hope opens the veil and binds us to Jesus, and when thus bound, faith grows. Since faith comes by hearing and hearing by the Word, it is only logical that faith must grow when hope binds us to Jesus (the Word Himself).

Here's another summary of how it works:

Hope enters the veil.

Hope puts down an anchor and keeps us there.

Hope binds us to the lover of our soul.

If we attach to His love, we'll be secure enough to hope *again*.

If we attach to hope, we'll eventually get faith.

If we attach to faith, we'll eventually get a breakthrough.

Where are you in this cycle? If you can practice these principles, you'll receive a song of ascents to sing to a struggling world. Carry on! The lover of your soul awaits!

11

Hold Me Tight

They were the best of friends; they were the worst of friends!

Up to this point, I have focused on you personally and your challenges, but what do you need *from your friends* when tragedy gives you a front-row seat in the story of Job? What do you do if you suddenly find that *you* are a friend of a modern-day Job? In this chapter, I would like to outline some very practical truths that we can apply in our friendships with those who are suffering the pain of loss or tragedy or disappointment.

We desperately need friends, because, as we've seen from the preceding chapters, it is not easy to respond biblically to heartache. The insights and suggestions are often vague and challenging. They are vague because grief is so unique for the individual suffering from it, and they are challenging because the mere act of breathing can seem like a Herculean task for a bereaved soul. It is terribly difficult to know how to respond to grief, and by the way, the grieving person is often the worst judge of his or her own emotional health and progress. Since the strategies and exhortations are quite challenging, let's zero in on the ones who sustain the hurting souls: their friends. Let's discuss the biblical response to the grief *of a friend*.

I'd like to examine this tender topic against the greatest backdrop of friendship in Scripture: the three friends of Job. Oh, I know some think they were awful friends, but if I'm ever a modern-day Job, I want them as my comforters. Yes, some say they were the worst of friends, but we will discover that they were also the very best of friends.

Before we explore the vices and virtues of Job's friends, let's review a basic scriptural truth regarding friendship and grief. Romans 12:15 tells us to *"Weep with those who weep."* God doesn't want anyone weeping alone. In fact, it's impossible to do so. Even if we desire isolation or if we feel forsaken, we *can't* grieve alone. If my friend is grieving, his grief is now a part of our friendship, and our relationship has changed whether I like it or not. It's changed whether I know what to say or not. It's changed even if I hate the change.

It's not easy to know how to be a friend in times of crisis, but it's crucial that we learn. A grieving individual may need counsel, but they don't live with their counselor; they live life with their friends. Your faithful friendship may very well save the destiny of your friend.

Proverbs 18:24 says, *"There is a friend who sticks closer than a brother."* This verse is supposed to blow us away with the fact that the Lord could actually be closer than our brother or friend; but what happens if I'm not close to my brother and someone tells me that the Lord sticks closer than him? I may not be moved to tears at the prospect. This Scripture was inspired by the Holy Spirit on the assumption that godly men and women would know how to befriend a hurting world. He assumed they would so reflect His own compassionate, loyal nature that when this particular promise came (that He would stay even closer than them), a ministry would occur in the troubled soul. The quality of our relationships determines the power of this verse.

When asked to comment on the virtue of friendship, Morris said this:

> When a man, blind from his birth, was asked what he
> thought the sun to be like, he replied, "Like friendship."
> He could not conceive of anything more fitting as a

similitude for what he had been taught to regard as the most glorious of material objects, and whose quickening and exhilarating influences he had rejoiced to feel. And truly friendship is a sun, if not the sun, of life.[23]

What about the man who has no friend or brother? Ecclesiastes 4:8 reveals some things about this man. *"There was a man all alone; he had neither son nor brother. There was no end to his toil"* (NIV). A man with no child or brother has no end to his labor. The word *labor* means the unsatisfied feeling of being on a treadmill. Have you ever felt that way? I have. The word also implies a monotonous, gloomy discouragement. I've been there too. If you feel this way, it may be fair to ask the question: Are you imparting life and hope and friendship to a brother or son?

The power of friendship is one of the greatest powers on the planet. To cross the finish line of faith strong at my life's end, I'm going to need a friend. I'll probably need him more than I'll need a prophetic word. I desperately want to be that friend, too. I want to anchor my faith to someone so that they enter Heaven on account of my stubborn loyalty to their cause.

I know that Jesus aptly described our neighbor as any individual in need who crosses our path. I know that, as Christians, we are called to be salt and light wherever we are, and that we should love and encourage hundreds of people in our lifetime. I also believe, however, that each of us may have one or two opportunities in our lifetime to actually be used by God to help save the destiny of another. I believe there is someone who, very literally, may not make it without you. I know I wouldn't have made it alone.

I'm not writing this from a position of great personal fortitude and determination. I'm not well onto my recovery (and I am) by my great individual response to God's grace. My friends carried me most of the way. I may have dangled a toe on the pavement occasionally as we crossed, but that's about all I've done to carry on.

Thank you, Todd, for holding me tight in the backseat of your car when I broke down like a baby in the movie theatre that day. The vivid pictures of a father's love for his child in that movie were too graphic for my newly broken soul.

Thank you, Bruce, for making me laugh when I was just certain that the world was indeed a mean street.

Thank you, Floyd, for never allowing a church service to conclude without grabbing me and telling me that your faith for me was still strong.

Thank you, Roy, for crying with me in your hot tub.

Thank you, Mike, for being there within minutes of our midnight call.

Thank you, Randy, for spending your evenings outside the window of the NICU pleading with God for mercy.

Thank you, Gayle and Cindy, for remembering.

Thank you, Scott and Dawn, for desiring to know.

Thank you, Amber Lee, for always caring.

Thank you, Holy Spirit, for sticking closer than a brother. Oh, Lord, make me a friend!

Well, let's tackle Job. Before we examine his friends with all their raw humanity, let me make a few general comments about the story of Job and his extreme suffering. I don't believe that Job is an untouchable book. I believe we *can* understand its resident truths. It is very true that some events on planet Earth do baffle the human mind, but we should grapple with them anyway. Why do bad things happen to good people? Such questions may never be fully answered here on this side of Heaven, but I believe we should still wrestle through them. Who knows, if we wrestle with a big question, we just might receive a big answer.

The Book of Job can shake our theology. It's encouraging because we think, *If Job survived his nightmare, then I can survive mine as well.* However, it's also discouraging because God allowed it to happen. *If Job was so righteous and holy and God still let him experience tragedy, what about me?* Tough question. Let me respond by saying that, first and foremost, Job is a book of worship. It is a book about costly worship in the face of the unthinkable.

Most scholars believe that the Book of Job was the first book written in Scripture and that the timeline of the events of the book occurred prior to Abraham. If this is true, and Moses did indeed pen its pages before he wrote, "In the beginning" in Genesis, then we can see a powerful truth from the Holy Spirit: The law of first mention *for the Bible itself* shows how we are to worship God regardless of what life or the devil or humanity brings our way. Job is a book of worship. From the beginning chapters when he fell on his face and declared his dependence on God, until its final pages when he offered another sacrifice, Job teaches us how to worship.

Job was a true worshipper, and he was the most righteous man of his day. In fact, he is listed with Enoch for his godliness. Why, then, would God allow the devil to have a heyday with this man?

We can get freaked out because the initial chapters of the book give us a behind-the-scenes look at a dialogue between God and satan. God seems almost flippant about the horrific tragedies that befall His "servant Job" seemingly at satan's mere request. I spoke with a man once who said he would become a Christian if only he could reconcile the Book of Job in his thinking. "Why," he asked me, "would God allow His best man to be devastated because of a bet with the devil?" I don't mean to deviate too much from our theme of befriending those in grief, but please let me share my response to this question.

How many of you reading these words have taken comfort at some point in your life from the story of Job? How many of you have purposed to endure the dark night of your soul because Job endured his? How many of you have vowed along with Job,

"Though He slays me, yet I will trust Him"? You're not alone in your vow.

At the end of the story, the Book of Job says, *"Then all his brothers, all his sisters, and all those who had been his acquaintances before, came to him..."* (emphasis added). Because the beginning of the book tells us that he was the richest man of the east, we can safely assume that he was acquainted with thousands of people. A thousand people in his own day heard of his heart toward God! A thousand people heard how the Lord restored his fortune. Today, billions of people have heard the story.

When God said to satan, "Have you considered My servant Job?" He was not callously thrusting Job into the fire—He was declaring war on satan! "Have you considered My servant Job?" Satan's second worst mistake was to answer that question. (His worst mistake was to crucify Jesus at Golgotha.)

Think with me. If Job had never suffered, his book would have been only five verses long. We would know that he was rich and righteous and loved by God, and then we'd go looking for a role model that we could more personally relate to. I can't relate to the richest and holiest man of the east. This attack by satan produced a weapon that has broken satanic attacks for centuries. Let me quickly add a disclaimer: Although tremendous good and encouragement came from Job's ordeal, it didn't make the bad good. His loss was excruciating. It was terrible, and I doubt he ever fully recovered from it.

Gerald Sittser in his book, *A Grace Disguised*, wrote: "The good that may come out of the loss does not erase its badness or excuse the wrong done. Nothing can do that."[24] I'm quick to add this thought because, believe it or not, good *will* someday come out of your experience. Someday your trauma will be an entry point to release hope to someone else, but when that happens, please don't falsely assume that God created the bad, so you could do some good. Remember from Genesis that everything God created was good. At the end of Genesis, Joseph said to his brothers, *"You meant evil against me; but God meant it for good"* (Gen. 50:20). God does not create the evil, but He does redeem it.

Tremendous good has come from my life with Alexis, but that good will never make the horror acceptable. What happened was tragic, and despite the good that may come of it, it will *never* be good. If we could settle the fact that we live in a sin-stricken world where bad things do, at times, happen to good people, we may experience more peace with less shaking of our theology. God is sovereign, and He will one day sum up all things in Jesus and dry every tear. However, His sovereignty does not mean that He *makes* everything happen as it does. He would never cause a rape or a betrayal or a rejection, but they happen every day. He has allowed man his free will, but He has promised to work the sum total of our experiences for good and to someday hold us tight and remove every sting and heartache.

Well, satan should have learned his lesson with Job. He certainly should have learned it from Jesus; but instead of learning from his mistakes, he now attacks you and me. The crucible you have experienced is very likely the crafting of some holy weapon that the Lord will someday wield to devastate the host of hell. You just need to survive the forging with the honesty and humility of Job.

One primary way to survive the fire is to walk with godly friends. No matter who we are, we need people. No matter how strong someone may seem or how well they may be coping with their trial, no one can make it alone. Not even Job.

Many people think that Job's friends cursed and mistreated him. We all share a little smirk when preachers mention "Job's comforters" and similar phrases. We're not totally unjustified in a little chuckling. After all, most of the book consists of their accusations against Job. It seemed obvious to them that if someone was experiencing so much freakish tragedy, they must have done something to deserve it. Somewhere in their life, they reasoned, this person must have ticked off Providence.

It is true that in some ways, the friends of Job didn't really help him. Remember with me, however, that in all of Job's testing, God never showed up until Job's friends did. Were they perfect friends? Did they say and do everything perfectly? No, and neither will you or I. They weren't perfect, but they were friends; and in all of Job's nine months of suffering, the Lord didn't speak until they spoke.

You may be thinking, *Well, the Lord showed up to rebuke them for their treatment of Job.* I'm not so sure. I'm more inclined to believe that the Lord was setting a precedent. Remember, Job is the first book of the Bible. In this book of first mentions, it is revealed to us that *our friends help us get to God.* Am I saying that the Lord won't intercede for us personally in our grief? No, but I am saying that the power of true friendship is unparalleled in times of heartache and disappointment. Friends have the power to reintroduce us to God.

Let's observe and experience their friendship. Job 2:11 says, *"Now when Job's three friends* [Eliphaz, Bildad, and Zophar] *heard…."* The Bible singles out these three men, but they weren't the only men present with Job. Job 32:1 says, *"So these three men ceased answering…"* (emphasis added). This written implication is that there were probably more than the three. We know from the story that at the very least, Elihu was also present. It's easy for us to picture these five men (including Job and Elihu) huddled up in the dust together, but it's likely that there were many more.

Job was a very important man. As the richest man of the east, he assuredly had hundreds of contacts and associates. He was probably sitting in the middle of a crowd who had gathered to see what would become of this righteous man who had experienced a near-mythical portion of bad luck. He was surrounded by people, but in the middle of the crowd, he had three friends. Aren't you glad for friends? You can be surrounded by people and still feel friendless. I want someone to say of me, "I had a lot of people in my life, but he was my friend!"

The first thing we notice about Job's friends is that they were distinct from the crowd. The crowd can give superb verbal counsel, but it's nothing compared to the arms of a friend. The crowd can pray and prophesy, and although we need those things, they're nothing compared to a friend who quietly holds you tight.

Job 2:11 says, *"Each one came from his own place"* (emphasis added). They were each unique. You can't be best friends with every person in your life, but God will link you with specific, unique people. Don't ever box in God in this area. You would probably be shocked if you could see the friends that He has in store for you. They're probably quite different from you. They may vary in age, personality, race, and certainly, in life experience. You would probably never choose them on your own; but they will lay their lives down for you, and you will love them like your own soul. True friends are like that.

Some of your Jonathan-and-David-type relationships will look very different from what you may imagine. By the way, did you know that Jonathan and David were of two different generations? When Jonathan's heart was knit with David, David was a very young man while Jonathan was a father in his 40's. I've had much older men in age become dear and treasured friends.

Well, how did Job's "big three" befriend him? They did seven things that proved their friendship and loyalty. If you and I can implement these seven attributes, we will truly be called brothers and sisters born for adversity.

At the end of Job's Book, we learn that practically everyone in that region had heard about him. But when these three men heard about the tragedy, they *"had made an appointment together to come and mourn with him"* (Job 2:11). They made an appointment to sit in a dusty road with their weeping comrade. Here, then, is the first key to befriending those in grief.

We must remember them.

This sounds so simple and so obvious, but it is so incredibly important. Remember your friends! Remember them even when your life moves on and you are swept up in the busyness that engulfs every life—every life, that is, except the life of the bereaved.

For the bereaved soul, there is far too much time. There is too much time to weep and to mourn and to remember. *You* remember *them!* Write them into your calendar so you won't forget. Often, in my personal calendar, I will write notes that say things like, "Remember that Mark is hurting this week," or "Send a card to Travis because it's been a month since he lost his mother." Even though I truly love my friends, I sometimes forget about them if I don't write it down. Make an appointment. Set a date to grieve.

Most friends and acquaintances are wonderful at the moment of initial loss. Their cards of sympathy are well-meaning and kind. Please continue this practice, but don't stop there. Send cards after funerals, but send them again a month or two later. Send more flowers after the initial wave has wilted and died, and then send a fresh bouquet a year later. Remember anniversaries and birthdays and special occasions. "They had made an appointment together to come and mourn with him."

Surprisingly, part of the definition of the word *appointment* means a congregation assembling to worship God. For the friends of Job, their appointment with his grief was a holy priority. Let me say it this way: They made it a holy priority to remember.

This convicts me. I often hear of hardships that befall those whom I love, and although I really do care, I am very quickly caught up in my own world of busyness and stress until I eventually forget. I may see them a few weeks later in church or the supermarket where I encourage them, wish them well, and secretly recommit to remember.

Galatians 6:2 tell us to bear one another's burdens. This is a wonderful admonition, but when we bear *another's* burden, we must remember it is another's burden. As much as you truly care and as greatly as you desire to help, *they* are the ones living with the burden, not you.

When I carry a burden for someone, it goes something like this: I am introduced to the need via a request for help, a personal observation, or a direct prompting from the Lord. Once I sense the burden, I respond by making a phone call, writing a card, or praying. After a time of prayer, I will usually receive a sense of the Lord's peace and presence. I make a mental note to follow up with the individual at a later date. Then I forget.

This process that I've just described is not a bad process. In fact, many times it's probably exactly how the Lord wanted me to respond. My point in mentioning this is to say that, while I may feel a breakthrough and a release fairly quickly, the friend for whom I am interceding is still carrying the burden. We're limited in how much we can actually carry one another's burdens. No matter how much we would like to empathize, we can only get so far into someone else's shoes. One of the best ways to serve them in their burden-bearing is simply to remember that the burden is still weighing heavily on their bowed shoulders. Jesus does this.

He was touched with all the feelings of our infirmities so He could identify with every one of us in our hour of need. He really does know how we feel, and He really is able to stick closer than a brother.

Psalm 103 is a fantastic psalm that beautifully captures the Lord's love and commitment to us. Amidst the list of all the great things He does for us, like forgiving sin, renewing our youth, and crowning us with loving kindness, verse 14 says that He also remembers our frame. He remembers us! He remembers that we are dust. He remembers that we are fragile and in need of a loving Savior. I'm not sure which is more profound: the fact that He forgives our sin, or that He simply remembers us. While ruling and reigning over the universe, He remembers that you and I are struggling, and He releases the mercy of a kind father.

Job's friends remembered him, but they didn't stop there. They acted on their remembrance of him. They made an appointment to *mourn with him*. After they remembered his state, their first priority was simply to hold his hand and cry. They demonstrated the greatness of their relationship when they came, not to comfort or to counsel, but to weep with him in his weeping. They didn't immediately go to Scripture and try to explain how good would come from the tragedy. They didn't immediately share how God likes to walk with His servants in their fiery furnaces. They didn't try to get Job to see the big picture. They just wanted to sit in the dirt and look him deeply in the eyes and say, "Job, we love you, and since your world has changed, ours has too. We're here, and we are not leaving." Oh to have and to be a friend like that! This, then, is the second step in befriending the grieving.

We must mourn with them.

It's not easy to sit in silence in the presence of grief. Grief is unnerving. It's terribly awkward. In the moments of extreme heartache, there is no right thing to say. It's human nature to want to help our friends in these situations by offering a bit of wisdom and perspective. Please don't. Please just sit in the dirt and be present. Our Scripture tells us that the grief of Job was so profound that these men sat in silence *for seven days*.

I took a struggling friend to lunch once. He was having a Jonah day. He was angry and tired and hurting, and he felt as though he was wading in fish vomit. I sat in awkward silence for nearly two hours as he shared his heart. When I dropped him off at his house, I said, "I'm really sorry, but I don't feel like I helped you." His reply was swift and convicting. He said, "I didn't need help; I needed a friend."

Pride says: "I must have an answer. I must know what to do."

Love says: "I simply must be."

When our friends hurt, we are confronted with our own weaknesses and helplessness. It is especially difficult for a spouse or a parent. Spouses and parents are protectors and helpers and defenders, but sometimes there is nothing we can do. Sometimes we can only be. This is why Psalm 46 was written. After a description of warfare and strife and struggle, the Lord speaks in verse 10, *"Be still, and know that I am God."* Isn't it interesting that the Lord doesn't begin to unravel the mysteries of the universe. He simply says, "I am God. I am here and that is enough."

Ecclesiastes 3:7 says, "[There is] *a time to keep silence, and a time to speak."* The initial stages of grief are times for silence.

Let me clarify this thought for a moment, because I'm not referring to *literal* silence. The silence I am referencing is a refraining from the desire to fix the situation. We *do* need to speak. If you have a friend who is hurting, please, speak up. A fumbling, stammering "I love you" is much better than a biting of your tongue for fear of saying the wrong thing. If your loved one is in the throes of hard grief, you probably *will* say the wrong thing. When I was hurting and bleeding in my soul after losing my sweet daughter, I was angry when people didn't call, and I was angry and irritated when they did. How dare they forget me! Then, how dare they interrupt my pain! Oh, it's truly impossible to be the perfect friend. Let's drop the perfect and just be a friend.

These friends of Job sat in silence for seven days. These men had incredible humility. (I'll prove it before this chapter is finished.) They were incredibly wise men, learned and knowledgeable about God. They were fitting friends for a man like Job; and yet they reigned in their desire to fix the situation, and they sat in humble silence for an entire week.

After they sat in silence, they *"saw that his grief was very great"* (Job 2:13). By sitting in silence, they were able to accurately discern the degree of his pain. If they had jumped immediately to counsel, they would have missed the delicate heart of the matter. The hearts of the hurting need to be loved and remembered. Counsel will come later. The seven steps to recovery will come later. Early on, please, just love. Just sit.

Well, when the week ended, the situation instantly became more difficult for Job's friends, because when Job opened his mouth after a long week of awkward silence, he cursed the day of his birth. This leads us to the third step in comforting the grieving.

We must accept their humanity.

Only Jesus endured His crucible without sin. Don't expect your friends to be Jesus. You be Jesus for them! Let them grieve. Let them be real. Don't be intimidated if they become angry with God. The Lord was big enough to handle Job's anger, and He's big enough to handle theirs as well. Jeremiah cursed the day of His birth, and the Lord never even bothered to respond to it. God's confidence in us does not rest in our commitment to Him but in His commitment to us. Our covenant with Him is not based on our faltering faith but on His immutability—the unchangeableness of His nature.

In an earlier chapter, I admonished the grieving to trust their relationship with the Lord, and now I do the same for you, their friends. Trust God! Take a position of faith for your friend. Pain will addle their senses. They will say things today that they won't mean a year from now, but it's okay for them to be real. I'm not advocating an acceptance or toleration of sin, but I am emphatically saying that you, as the friend to a hurting comrade, must be a safe place for them to grieve. If they aren't thinking clearly, think for them. If their faith wavers, just remember the fellow with palsy who couldn't get to Jesus on his own and had to be "carried by four men" (Mk. 2:3). Be one of the four.

The fourth way to comfort the grieving is simply this.

We must comfort them.

The comfort began when the friends showed up, and it continued when they sat in silence for a week. There *will* be a time, however, for comfort through verbal encouragement. Let me point out here that, although I am listing a sequence of ministry to our grieving friends, there isn't an exact timetable to follow. We can't say, "Last week I listened, so this week I will counsel." We must be incredibly sensitive to the guidance of the Holy Spirit. There is one thing that we should dutifully follow, however, and that is a commitment to error on the side of sensitivity in our comforting conversations.

In *Everyday Comfort,* Randy Becton offers this wonderful advice to those who are consoling the hurting:

Remember that answers are only partial and mostly inadequate when the heart is broken.

Life and loss remain profound mysteries.

Comfort comes from unexpected sources, usually in quiet, simple ways.

The path to survival requires many reminders from the loving, caring God who grieves with you in life's darkest hours.[25]

To the hurting, Becton offers this suggestion of what to say to our friends in these moments:

Consider telling your friends, "I'm grieving, but I've never had to face a loss exactly like this. Stay close, but don't say too much unless I ask. I just want you to be a strong, mostly silent support system for me. I don't want to feel I'm losing my marbles. So help me, and somehow we'll make it through. I love you. You mean a lot to me. Just don't rush me, okay?"[26]

Grieving people are extremely vulnerable. Isaiah 42:3 contains the tender promise that the Lord will not break a bruised reed. Let's make sure we don't break them either. The Lord wants the hurting to be restored so let's ask Him for huge doses of His heart and His compassion. Let's do our best to refrain from speaking until we have discernment from the Lord. For our words to do any good for a discouraged soul, they must be words in season. They must be living words. Job's friends did great up until this point. They were the best of friends—until they spoke without discernment.

A terrible misconception we can practice is to think that if we have had a similar experience as the hurting individual is having, we know exactly how they feel. Of course, it's true that if you've walked in my shoes, you can understand a great deal of what I am experiencing. It's also true, however, that you will probably be limited to the paradigm of your similar experience. You may indeed be able to relate to my pain, but what comforted you may be an affliction to me.

Just because we may have shared similar experiences with our hurting friends does *not* mean we automatically have the wisdom of the Lord for them. We must ask the Lord for a relevant, living word for their situation. The Lord may want to minister to a different area in their life than He did in yours. He may be after something in them that He didn't need to bother with in you.

This admonition may seem too obvious to warrant mentioning, but it must still be said: Whatever you do in comforting a sorrowful friend, do *not* say, "I know exactly how you feel." When my firstborn daughter was fighting for her life in the neo-natal intensive care unit, several well-intentioned friends made statements like, "I can relate to your situation because my cousin was a few weeks premature and had to stay in the NICU for three weeks," or "I know just how you feel because my grandmother has been in the hospital a lot recently." Please hear my heart—I'm not at all offended or critical, but these individuals didn't have the slightest clue what it is like to watch their baby fight for her life. An aged grandmother or a distant cousin is not a daughter. Please hear this as well: A daughter is not a cousin or a grandmother. Losing a daughter is worse than having a cousin born three weeks premature (and still living today), but even if my grief seems worse, it does not invalidate yours. I can't imagine anything worse than losing a child, but I've never lost my spouse. I've never felt the betrayal and the soul-crushing force of a divorce. Darkness is darkness; and I can relate to your raw emotion, but I can't relate specifically to you. Nor can you relate to me. A wise friend accepts this and proceeds with great care.

Job's friends judged by what they saw, not by what they heard. They *saw* that his grief was very great, but they didn't *hear* what the Lord was saying about his grief. They saw a man who was cursing his birth, but they didn't hear the heart of the Lord for that cursing man. Their counsel was largely scriptural. Most of what they said can be cross-referenced and substantiated by other Scriptures. However, Jesus said in John 5:30, "*As I hear, I judge.*" If we don't stop to listen to Him, we might *see* judgment when He is *saying* mercy. Those with similar experiences are especially vulnerable to this judgment. The commonality of their backgrounds makes them feel that they know what to say.

Job's friends didn't have an answer, but they felt compelled to say something. In Job 5:8, Eliphaz said, essentially, "If it were me, I would seek God." Eliphaz, it's not you! Statements like that one only contain life if God genuinely inspires them. You don't need to relate to me to comfort me. You don't need to have lost a child to comfort me. You only need to love me. You only need to remember me and express your remembrance with sensitivity and kindness.

The first time I tried to console a family upon the death of a loved one, I felt inept at comforting them. On my way to their house, I felt confident that I could be a great source of solace since I had, in a sense, been in their shoes. When I arrived, however, and my own memories surfaced, I remembered how inadequate my words really are. Words *do* need to be spoken. Hope *does* need to be expressed, but it should be expressed with extreme care. This is especially true in light of the next point.

We must speak the truth to them.

Job's friends spoke the truth. It may not have been exactly what the Lord was saying to Job at that moment, but there were elements of truth in their counsel. They were wrong to speak without hearing first, but they weren't wrong to speak. I want my friends to be gentle with me, but I want them to speak. I want them to be under authority and submitted in their counsel, but I want them to speak up. I want to know that they love me, but I also want to know that they love me too much to let my grief destroy me. I don't want to walk off the edge of a cliff. Speak to me! Be a friend to me and speak the truth in love.

We must practice humility.

In Job 42:7-8, the Lord rebuked the three friends and gave them instructions for repentance. Verse nine says, *"Eliphaz...Bildad...and Zophar... went, and did according as the Lord commanded them"* (KJV). Really, we couldn't ask for better friends than these humble, obedient men. They remembered Job. They sacrificed the time, energy, and money it required to spend a week with him in silence. They mourned with him. They spoke the truth—they loved him enough to be honest with him. They instantly repented when it was shown that they were wrong. Oh, I want to be a friend like that!

Job 42:10 says that the Lord turned the captivity of Job when he prayed for *his friends*. At the end of the book, they were still his friends! I like the preceding verse 9. It says, *"...[they] did according as the Lord commanded them: the Lord also accepted Job"* (KJV, emphasis added). That word also implies that the Lord had accepted the three friends' obedience and repentance.

We must rejoice with them when the tide turns.

The tide will turn! Job 42:12 says, "*So the Lord blessed the latter end of Job more than his beginning*" (KJV).

Job might not have survived without Eliphaz, Bildad, and Zophar. Their friendship was crucial for his restoration. Indeed, God didn't show up until they came on the scene. Billions of people (including me) have needed Job to survive.

How do we befriend those in grief and assist in their recovery?

We must remember them.

We must mourn with them.

We must accept their humanity.

We must comfort them.

We must speak the truth to them.

We must humble ourselves if we are wrong.

We must rejoice when the tide turns and a new day dawns. Who knows, our friendship might just hasten that dawn.

Can you see them? Job, Eliphaz, Bildad, and Zophar are walking arm in arm into the sunset. This looks like the beginning of a beautiful friendship!

12

Spiritual Midwives

There are some dreams and desires that cannot be birthed alone. I attended a memorial service a couple years ago that changed my life and emphasized the truth of the above statement.

The service was held in the honor of a tremendous man of God who had valiantly battled cancer for several years. He had lived a life rich in the service of humanity. Many people spoke and lauded him with the praise that he was certainly due. One man in particular caught my attention and, subsequently, changed my life. He was a large, bear of a man—a medical doctor who had been deeply touched and blessed by the deceased. He rose to speak with a trembling voice and tearstained cheeks. His opening statement went off like fireworks in my spirit and has become the motivating cry for the remainder of my life. He said, "This man [the deceased] was always a midwife for my dreams."

A midwife for my dreams. Wow! What a statement! What a concept. It became my life's prayer and my life's dream to be remembered that way. I want to help birth the dreams of others. In the preceding chapter, we discussed the anatomy of a true friend. Here, let's take the study a step further and evaluate the heart of a spiritual midwife.

One night, Jessica and I encountered a spiritual midwife disguised as a natural physician. During one of Alexis' frequent bouts with pneumonia, our home health care nurse became alarmed and frightened with the severity of her condition, so we opted to hospitalize her rather than attempt treatment in our home. We had been to the pediatric intensive care unit many times, and all the nurses knew the drill. When we arrived, they asked us if we wanted the on-call doctor to evaluate Alexis even though we all knew what the diagnosis and prescribed treatment would be. We said that, yes, we still wanted him to see her, so they called the doctor, who was sleeping with his family, and we waited.

When he arrived on the floor of the pediatric intensive care unit, I eavesdropped on him. When a man is awakened from a peaceful sleep in the pre-dawn hours of the night, you see his true colors, and I wondered how he would respond. He didn't know I was watching him, but his response to my daughter forever won my heart. His first spoken words as he arrived on the floor were these: "So where is our little lady in waiting?" Oh, I love that man! What a response! That's the heart of a spiritual midwife.

Genesis 35:16-17 relates the story of Rachel and her midwife. It says, "*Then they journeyed from Bethel. And when there was but a little distance to go to Ephrath, Rachel labored in childbirth, and she had hard labor. Now it came to pass, when she was in hard labor, that the midwife said to her, 'Do not fear; you will have this son also.'*" Every hurting person needs a spiritual midwife. Let's stroll through these verses and identify eight traits of spiritual midwives that we can implement as we serve our hurting and struggling friends.

Spiritual midwives share the dreams of others.

The first thing that stands out to me is the phrase, "*Then they journeyed.*" The midwife traveled with them. She became part of the family. You can't become family as an itinerant midwife. How many mothers invite perfect strangers to observe the birth and delivery of their children? Of course, many of the nurses are strangers, but they are there by assignment, not personal invitation. I can't imagine a pregnant woman meeting a stranger in a grocery store and saying "Hey, I'm going to give birth on Thursday; would you like to come and watch?" She would never find someone in the shopping mall and ask, "Would you please feed me ice chips and rub my lower back during my labor and delivery this month?" Of course, the very thought of this is preposterous. Birthing, whether natural or spiritual, is a very private, personal event. The traveling minister who visited our church and preached insightful sermons wasn't my primary labor coach. The ones who helped me birth my dreams were the ones who lived and laughed and cried with me. The heart of a midwife says, "I want to be a part of your family. I don't want to merely give you a prescription for your pain; I want to hold your hand."

Spiritual midwives come to be after long, committed relationships. One of the beautiful things about Christianity is that brothers can be born in an instant at the altar, but in general, life-long friendships happen over a lifetime. We must join one another's families.

"*Rachel labored.*" If you're going to be a spiritual midwife, you're going to have to hang around pregnant people. I know that sounds so obvious, you are probably wondering why I said it. If you haven't been around a pregnant woman lately, let me remind you of some things. They have strange cravings at strange hours. They're always uncomfortable. They have trouble breathing at times because their internal organs are being squeezed and repositioned by the new little life inside them. They can't sleep as well as before, so they tire more easily. Pregnancy changes the way they walk. It changes the way they look. I think my wife was darling when she was pregnant. Did she think so? Certainly not.

Spiritual midwives are courageous.

Rachel was pregnant with more than a baby. She was carrying a dream. She was carrying a miracle. Dreaming is hard work.

If you conceive the life of God and His dream grows inside of you, you're in for some changes. You'll have to alter your lifestyle to care for your dream. Jessica had to give up coffee. Miraculous dreams aren't easy to carry. They invite spiritual opposition. It's probably worth mentioning that if you aspire to the station of spiritual midwife, you'll probably get tangled up in some spiritual warfare before the delivery is complete.

Satan wants to crush your dreams before they are conceived. He wants to so wound and discourage and disappoint you that you give up on dreaming. He wants you to say, "I had a dream—and it was shattered! Dreams come true only in Walt Disney movies!"

If a dream *is* conceived in you, satan will try to invoke a miscarriage through circumstances that wear you down until you give up on your dream. Jessica miscarried a pregnancy two months prior to conceiving Madelyn. Miscarriages can be very painful for the expectant mother. It's not the loss of what was, but the loss of what might have been. This can be excruciating for some parents. It's a similar pain to barrenness.

If satan can't invoke a miscarriage or seduce you into performing an abortion of your dream, and you carry this spiritual child full-term, you're still not out of the woods. Revelation 12:4 says, "*The dragon stood before the woman who was ready to give birth, to devour her Child as soon as it was born.*" There is great risk in dreaming. There is the risk that the dream might not come true.

You're not alone in this risk. God took a huge risk by placing His dreams within the hearts of men and women. Think of it! There are God-ideas and God-dreams living inside you. If *your* dreams come true, *His* Kingdom will increase on planet Earth, and Heaven will need to add another section of bleachers for the saints who will eventually join the great cloud of witnesses as a result of your faithfulness.

R. Wayne Willis told this story of Louis Pasteur:

Louis Pasteur, the pioneer of immunology, lived at a time when thousands of people died each year of rabies. Pasteur had worked for years on a vaccine. Just as he was about to begin experimenting on himself, a nine-year-old, Joseph Meister, was bitten by a rabid dog. The boy's mother begged Pasteur to experiment on her son. Pasteur injected Joseph for ten days—and the boy lived.

Decades later, of all the things Pasteur could have had etched on his headstone, he asked for three words: JOSEPH MEISTER LIVED.[27]

Someone will live as a result of your faithfulness to the Lord!

I said that Rachel was carrying a dream, but her dream was actually a miracle. Do you remember that she was barren previously? It was a merciful miracle from the Lord that she had even conceived and carried the child this far. For years, she was barren just like Sarah and Rebekah. Genesis 30:1 reveals her grief. She said to Jacob, *"Give me children, or else I die!"* What anguish and despair of soul. Look at the following sequence of events in verses 2-8 to see the depth of her pain.

Jacob became angry with her and said, "Am I in the place of God, who has kept you from having children?" Then she said, "Here is Bilhah, my maidservant. Sleep with her so that she can bear children for me and that through her I too can build a family." So she gave him her servant Bilhah as a wife. Jacob slept with her, and she became pregnant and bore him a son. Then Rachel said, "God has vindicated me; He has listened to my plea and given me a son." Because of this she named him Dan. Rachel's servant Bilhah conceived again and bore Jacob a second son. Then Rachel said, "I have had a great struggle with my sister, and I have won." So she named him Naphtali (Genesis 30:2-8 NIV).

She said, "I have had a great struggle...and I have won"; but she still hadn't personally conceived. It was a shallow mockery of a victory. Her struggle had produced no life. Oh, but look at the mercy of God in verses 22-24. *"Then God remembered Rachel; He listened to her and opened her womb. She became pregnant and gave birth to a son and said, 'God has taken away my disgrace.' She named him Joseph, and said, 'May the Lord add to me another son.'"* I love it! God remembered Rachel, and He gave her Joseph. Wasn't he the one who grew up to become a famous dreamer? Didn't he dream and interpret some dreams that saved a nation?

The Lord listened to her and remembered her. The word *listened* means to give one's undivided listening attention to someone. She had the undivided attention of Heaven. Effective midwives pay attention to their laboring companions, and they remember their dreams.

Spiritual midwives aren't afraid of tears.

I would wager that our midwife wept bitter tears when she saw Rachel's pain and when she watched Jacob enter the tent of Bilhah.

Rachel gave birth to Joseph whose name meant "the Lord will add." The Lord *did* add another son and back in Genesis 35:16 we read that *"Rachel labored"* and it was *"hard labor."* The word *hard* in this Scripture means cruel, severe, and fierce. It takes fierce labor to birth certain dreams. In fact, I believe any dream worth birthing will require fierce labor to bring it forth. Some of those painful, spiritual contractions you've been feeling are not necessarily indicators that you are out of God's will— they could be signs that you're about to give birth.

Spiritual midwives must be ready in and out of season.

One of the problems with fierce labor is that you don't always know when it will begin. Oh, you have a due date. Jessica required c-section deliveries with all our girls. With Amber and Madelyn, we literally set the date for their births, but, typically, you never really know for sure when the baby's coming. Your dreams can come true suddenly! It's an exhilarating thought. When Peter and the boys had fished all night and caught nothing, they had no idea that a miracle was only one more cast away. Keep casting! The blessing could break your nets anytime now.

Spiritual midwives are highly flammable.

They carry gasoline, not water. They are always ready to pour gas on the fiery dreams of others. Spiritual midwives fuel the dreams of others because they are dreamers themselves. They dream that the dreams of others will come true. What a noble calling.

Spiritual midwives speak a very specific language.

In verse 17, as Rachel travailed in fierce labor, the midwife spoke, *"Do not fear; you will have this son also."* You can always tell a midwife by their speech. They say things like:

"Fear not!"

"I believe in you!"

"You will have this child also!"

"You're not losing this son!"

"You will give birth to this dream!"

"You're not going to die in transition!"

"What did God say to you? I agree with you!"

"Let's agree together in prayer right now."

"What's your dream? You want to be president of the United States? Well, reserve me a seat at your inauguration."

God wants to scream to you from the heavens, "I believe in you! You will have this son also! I know you feel like you're camping out in hell, but I will bring you into a good place."

Sometimes He likes to send this message to you via spiritual midwives.

Spiritual midwives are people of faith.

They believe in God's grace working through humanity.

Spiritual midwives carry peace.

You who would be spiritual midwives, be sure to wear surgical gloves and a mask around the dreams of others. They can be very fragile. Do you know that a raised eyebrow can crush a dream? A snicker or a sneer can be a death sentence to the dream of another (especially in children). No one wants a chatterbox in the delivery room with them. When they do speak, they say, "Fear not." Midwives carry peace.

If you have read this story on your own and skipped to the end, you know that Rachel died during this delivery. Can I take a little liberty with the text? In the KJV, verse 18 says her soul was departing. Conceiving, carrying, and birthing God's dreams will kill certain parts of our soul. Life can't go on as usual with a baby dream from God. I realize I'm misapplying this particular Scripture, but this principle is widely supported all throughout the Bible. He's got to deal with our sin nature. John the Baptist said it this way: *"He must increase, but I must decrease"* (Jn. 3:30).

In this process of decreasing we cry out like Rachel, *"His name is Ben-Oni."* She named this added son *Ben-Oni*, which means the son of my sorrow. At this point in the birthing process, we are in trouble. We desperately need a midwife (who is a type of the Holy Spirit).

In the Greek language, the Holy Spirit was called the *paraklete. Paraklete* is one called alongside to help. A midwife sits alongside and cheers you on, but remember that *you* have to give birth. The midwife is not a surrogate mother; they're a cheerleader. If your midwife wants it more badly than you do, it won't happen.

As areas of your soul depart and something new takes its place in you, you must be reminded that this is not the fruit of your sorrow. This son is not Ben-Oni. Jacob said, "*His name is Benjamin.*" *Benjamin* means the son of my right hand. The right hand typified power, strength, and might in Scripture. What God is producing in you is from His right hand. Who sits at the right hand of God? Jesus! As you allow your soul to depart, Jesus is formed in you.

I know you're hurting right now, but I want you to know that you will heal. In a few months or years, you'll be unrecognizable—you'll look more like Him. Fear not, you're going to have this dream also!

Be a friend to those in crisis, but take your friendship to a deeper level and commit to serve as their midwife. When hell is screaming in their face, hold their hand and whisper in their ear, "Fear not!"

I know we have been discussing *spiritual* midwives in this chapter, but let me conclude by releasing a blessing on *natural* physicians. The nurses and doctors who served me, Jessica, and Alexis in our time of need were truly Heaven-sent. Some were Christians, some were not; but most all of them were Jesus to us. They loved our daughter, and they served her well. Thank you! Thank you and bless you to all of the caring individuals who have devoted their lives to the practice of medicine for the purpose of alleviating the suffering of the world.

Greg Asimakoupoulos in *Leadership Journal* told a story of a modern-day midwife for the dream of another. He wrote:

In the summer of 1989, Mark Wellman, a paraplegic, gained national recognition by climbing the sheer granite face of El Capitan in Yosemite National Park. On the seventh and final day of his climb, the headlines of *The Fresno Bee* read, "Showing a Will of Granite." Accompanying the headline was a photo of Wellman being carried on the shoulders of his climbing companion Mike

Corbett. A subtitle said, "Paraplegic and partner prove no wall is too high to scale."

What many people did not know is that Mike Corbett scaled the face of El Capitan three times in order to help Mark Wellman pull himself up once.[28]

"He was a midwife for my dreams." If that becomes my epitaph, then, to quote Dr. Martin Luther King, Jr., "My living will not be in vain."

13

Still Shots

"*D*eath *is the destiny of every man and the living should take it to heart.*" So said the preacher in the Book of Ecclesiastes. He said this, not with a macabre, defeatist tone but with the perspective of a man who had come full circle in his life. "If I live my life from the grave looking back," he reasoned, "I would live a life of greater impact and significance. If I take to heart the end result and its accompanying big picture, I stand a better chance of surviving the loose ends of my life." The preacher had begun his journey asking hard questions, and he had concluded his search with simply this: *God.*

It's good to ask the hard questions, but to make any sense of them, we must ask them from a peculiar position: We must ask them from the grave looking back.

John M. Drescher, in *Pulpit Digest*, writes:

When John Owen, the great Puritan, lay on his deathbed his secretary wrote (in his name) to a friend, "I am still in the land of the living."

"Stop," said Owen. "Change that and say, 'I am yet in the land of the dying, but I hope soon to be in the land of the living.' "[29]

Some questions will never be answered until we enter the true land of the living.

Why didn't I receive a miracle when I was just certain that God had told me to fight for one?

Why do bad things happen to good people?

If He didn't come through for me *then*, how can I trust Him *now*?

Is the sovereignty of God merely a cop-out?

How should I then live?

These are valid questions that deserve answers, but they can never be answered with only a perspective from the present moment. They must be answered by the Ancient of Days. Life will not make sense until we see it from His perspective, and His perspective is the big picture.

Probably the greatest hurdle for Christians to overcome when they wrestle with these tough questions is their *present-moment perspective*. This present moment that we live in is only a fleeting dot on the span of eternity, and yet it is incredibly powerful. Although this present moment is merely a still shot of our life, we allow this brief, fleeting moment to shape our theology and our view of God. Something bad happens in this present moment, and we make a judgment against eternity. The Ancient of Days should never be judged by a mere moment in time. He doesn't judge *us* that way.

Some still shots are quite ugly. Ugly, awful, horrific things happen on planet Earth, and if our only perspective is the moment in which they happen, we are sunk. Although we live from ticking second to ticking second, we can't make our life judgments based on the reality of one moment. God usually does *not* work all things out for good immediately after tragedy occurs, but if we have the courage and the character to ascend to His heavenly, bird's-eye, big-picture perspective, we will see that He is able to conquer in and through still shots of even deep darkness.

Please don't judge me by the still shots of my life! If you wait a few seconds, you'll see another picture. One freeze-frame of my countenance is not the entire picture of my life. In one frame you might see some unattractive things. You might see some attitudes and thoughts that a Christian leader should *never* feel or think. Wait! There's another frame. In this one I might be repenting. In the next one, you might see me returning to God. If you wait for another shot, you might see me embracing destiny. This is the way God views us! He views us based on the final still shot, not merely the one that we are currently living. God looks at the sum total.

What if we judged King David based on single still shots of his life? What are some of the things that we would see? Selfishness. Lust. Pride. Envy. Murder. Deception. Would you want him for a king? Would you want him ministering to your family? How did God judge him? He said, "He's a man after My own heart."

When we meet David in Heaven, we won't say, "Oh, yeah, you were the adulterer, right?" Or "Didn't you have Uriah murdered?" No! We'll say, "David, thank you for paying the price! Thank you for staying in the process and allowing the Lord to heal you. I tried my best to follow your lead through my own valley of the shadow of death. You inspired me to carry on. Thank you, David!"

It does not matter what the individual still shots reveal. Sure, there was a picture of the prodigal son eating out of a pig sty far from his father's house, but that wasn't the end of his story. The final freeze-frame showed a ring on his finger and a robe on his shoulder as the father wept for joy at his return. I'll bet your final still shot is glorious!

You may not believe that, but it's true. I wish I could tell you all of the good that God will someday produce as a result of the hell you've experienced, but it probably wouldn't matter if I could. You might reject the words even if I had them. That's the problem with still shots. We can't see the final frame until we get there.

In Psalm 37, David wrote, *"I have been young, and now am old; yet I have not seen the righteous forsaken, nor his descendants begging bread"* (Ps. 37:25). David couldn't have written Psalm 37 as a young man. He needed the wisdom of one who had crossed the finish line and had seen God's provision.

In some of the still shots of our lives, we feel forsaken because everything looks like rejection. As a young man, I've seen a lot of rejection. I have to remind myself that I haven't seen the final frame yet.

Psalm 23 is another one. A common misconception is that David wrote it as a young shepherd boy while he was watching his father Jesse's sheep. While he certainly drew from his youthful experiences for the analogies of the psalm, he penned it as an old man.

This glorious psalm concludes with the bold statement, *"Surely goodness and mercy shall follow me all the days of my life...."* The word *surely* could also be translated "only." He said "Only goodness and mercy have followed me all the days of my life— even though some of those days took me through the valley of the shadow of death." During a dark season of his life, he had emerged from the valley of the shadow of death only to see goodness and mercy hot on his trail. How could David have written this as a young man?

From the perspective of the aged, David said, "I've seen it all. I've lived the good, the bad, and the ugly. I've been anointed, and I've wanted to die. I've experienced burnout, and I've feasted in the face of my foes. I'm about to die and enter His presence where I will dwell forever, and I have this final observation to make: In the final analysis of my life (from the sheepfold to the cave to the throne), it was only goodness and mercy that followed me from the Lord. Yes, it was *only* goodness and mercy that followed me!"

They're following *you*, too!

I'd like to conclude this brief chapter by sharing a beautiful still shot that I found one day as I was studying a Scripture from the Gospel of Luke. It's a Scripture that reveals a description of Heaven. I know your story is different from mine, and the trial you are surviving may not involve the death of a loved one. If it does, however, you may receive some comfort (as I did and still do) from this description that Jesus Himself gave of Heaven.

Luke 23:43 relays the familiar story of Jesus and the repentant thief on the cross. When this penitent sinner responded to the lordship of Christ, he received this promise from Jesus: "*Today, you will be with Me in Paradise.*" It's a simple statement, but it is rich in insight. "*Today, you will be **with Me**....*" We could end right there, and that would be enough. To be with Jesus! Could there be anything better? The only thing I can think of that might possibly be a little bit better would be being with Him *in Paradise*.

When Jesus said the word *Paradise*, He chose a wonderful old word that was used to describe a famous Mesopotamian king who had a passion for gardens. This king so loved gardens that, wherever he traveled, he commanded that a garden be constructed on the top of the building in which he would be staying. There were special instructions given to those who would build this garden: It was to contain everything beautiful that the earth could produce, and there was to be a strong wall around the perimeter of it to keep everything evil out. What a picture! Jesus said, "Today, you will be locked away *with Me* in a place where there is only beauty. Evil cannot penetrate this place."

The word also means *the place of future happiness and the paradise of God*. Revelation 2:7 says that those who return to their first love relationship with Jesus will eventually get to eat from the tree of life that grows in this paradise.

What a wonderful place! Your citizenship is there. Paradise is your destiny. Stay the course. You can do it. Someday you will be *with Him in Paradise.*

Alexis is there.

Someday, I'll be there too!

CONCLUSION

The Things That Remain

Paul commanded Titus to "*Set in order what remains* (Titus 1:5 NASB)." It's a good command, Paul, but it's much easier said than done. What are those things that remain? How do we begin? Through the course of our time together, I've made several assumptions about you and the things that remain. Let me share them with you.

I've assumed that you have pursued. I've assumed you have run hard after some good dreams. You've pursued a healing or a blessing or a relationship. You've sought the Lord for a break-through. You've been breathless and exhilarated and weary and elated. Whether or not you feel good about your race, I'm sure you've run well.

I assume you've pursued hard after the good things of God, but since you're reading this book, I also assume that you've come up short in areas of your pursuit. You have tried your best and you're still staring bankruptcy or divorce or bereavement in the face. You have prayed your guts out and now you wonder where God was and is.

I assume you feel like you may have failed. Should you have prayed harder? Should you have believed with a little more gusto? Perhaps your confession was a little too negative. Were you too selfish? Hear me: *You did not fail!*

I assume that your world looks different now. Mine sure does. The very landscape of your world has changed (even if you live in the same house you've owned for years). Even if you've driven the same streets for half your lifetime, it's probably a little harder to find your way home.

My next assumption is not an assumption at all but an irrefutable fact. I assume Jesus adores you. You may feel like a wreck. You may not even like the sight of yourself, but He is in love with you. He would rather visit you in your grief than parley with kings and emperors. He loves you!

Based on His love for you, His unquenchable power, and the resiliency that rests in your spirit, I also assume that you won't lay in your impotent state forever. I'm staking my claim on the assumption that you will live again. I believe you will be made whole. I believe you will love again. I don't believe you will die in your anguish. "Bitterly defeated" will not be your epitaph. I believe you will still give birth to the dreams of your heart.

I assume you have more compassion than you did before tragedy moved into your world. I assume you function with a deeper level of compassion and concern for mankind. You'll probably be a better friend than you were before. You'll probably be a better friend than you had yourself.

I assume that you now possess the heart of a spiritual midwife and that you're brave enough to hope again. I wish I knew you personally. I'm sure you're someone's hero.

So now what? Jessica and I received a wave of cards and notes and flowers when Alexis died. After a few weeks, they stopped coming. That's okay. Life moves on for the friends of the hurting, and that's not a bad thing—it's life. The problem for the hurting is that, for them, life seems to screech to a halt or, at best, the pace of a dying snail. When you feel stuck in suspended animation and the ache in your heart is worse three months *after* the initial loss, what do you do? How do you set things in order when you have no idea what those things are that require re-setting?

Let me try to help you. I know some things about you, and I can even tell you a few things that remain.

You remain. You're still here. You haven't quit yet, and that deserves a standing ovation. If you could see the angels now, I bet they're saluting you.

Your love remains. You wouldn't be hurting so badly if you didn't love. You haven't sealed off your heart with iron bars and concrete. Do you remember the old quote, "It's better to have loved and lost than never to have loved at all"? Do you agree with that? I do. It may not feel true when love has been lost, but, for me, it's a true sentiment. Four years later, I wouldn't bring Alexis Grace back to Earth from Heaven, but neither would I trade a day of her life. I would never choose a trial like this one, but I would never let someone take it away from me now that I've lived it. Every moment of my life with her was, and is, priceless. I'm reminded of Psalm 84:10 that says a day in the Lord's courts is better than a thousand outside. I calculated the math of those figures once so I could better relate to the thought, and I figured that the psalmist was saying that just one minute in the presence of the Lord is better than 16.67 hours anywhere else. I feel this way regarding Alexis. I miss her. And I'm not sure I will ever fully heal this side of Paradise, but I *will* live again.

Your faith remains. Remember, faith is the evidence of things not seen. You may see nothing positive in your experience (indeed there may be nothing positive in your experience). You may feel angry, cynical, and despairing; however, faith *does* remain because God still has faith in *you*.

Life remains. Even if your loss is bereavement like mine, life remains for you and the deceased. It's a thin veil that separates Heaven and earth. C.S. Lewis was so convinced of the reality of the afterlife that he referred to our existence on planet Earth as the shadow lands. If you aren't sure of your departed loved one's relationship with Jesus, trust that the Lord is merciful and that He alone knows the inner wrestling and vows of an individual's heart.

God remains. Gladys Aylward, missionary to China more than 50 years ago, was forced to flee when the Japanese invaded Yangcheng. However, she could not leave her work behind. With only one assistant, she led more than a hundred orphans over the mountains toward Free China.

In their book, *The Hidden Price of Greatness*, Ray Besson and Ranelda Mack Hunsicker tell what happened:

> During Gladys's harrowing journey out of war-torn Yangchen...she grappled with despair as never before. After passing a sleepless night, she faced the morning with no hope of reaching safety. A 13-year-old girl in the group reminded her of their much-loved story of Moses and the Israelites crossing the Red Sea.
>
> "But I am not Moses," Gladys cried in desperation.
>
> "Of course you aren't," the girl said, "but Jehovah is still God!"
>
> When Gladys and the orphans made it through, they proved once again that no matter how inadequate we feel, God is still God, and we can trust in Him.[30]

Jehovah *is* still God, and whether your pain is bereavement or the death of another dream, I say to you as well: *Life remains.* I know things have changed. You may walk differently for the rest of your earthly pilgrimage, but He's not finished with you yet. Be patient with yourself.

One of our young adult leaders preached a message at our church recently, and she shared how, during a very devastating time of her life, the Lord's only charge to her was this: "Just get in My presence and breathe." That's good advice. In fact, it's probably the best concluding advice I can offer. Get in His presence and breathe. If His presence seems absent, just sit tight. He won't leave you. The manifestation of His love and His goodness will be returned to you shortly. You can make it!

Fear not; you will live again!

Endnotes

1. Randy Becton, *Everyday Comfort* (Grand Rapids, MI: Baker Books, a division of Baker Book House Company, 1993), p. 38.

2. Ibid., p. 64.

3. Edward K. Rowell (editor), "Fresh Illustrations for Preaching and Teaching," *Leadership Journal* (Grand Rapids, MI: Christianity Today, Inc. and Baker Books, a division of Baker Book House Company, 1997), p. 169.

4. Josh McDowell, *The New Evidence That Demands a Verdict* (Dallas, TX: Thomas Nelson Publishers, 1999), p. 203.

5. Edward K. Rowell (editor), "Fresh Illustrations for Preaching and Teaching," *Leadership Journal* (Grand Rapids, MI: Christianity Today, Inc. and Baker Books, a division of Baker Book House Company, 1997), p. 8.

6. Ibid., p. 46.

7. C.S. Lewis, *A Grief Observed* (New York, NY: A Bantam Book/Published by Arrangement with The Seabury Press, Inc., 1976), p. 11

8. C. S. Lewis, *A Grief Observed*, p 41.

9. C. S. Lewis, *A Grief Observed*, p 66.

10. Wayne Willis (author) and Edward K. Rowell (editor), "Fresh Illustrations for Preaching and Teaching," *Leadership Journal* (Grand Rapids, MI: Christianity Today, Inc. and Baker Books, a division of Baker Book House Company, 1997), p. 124.

11. Ibid., p. 22.

12. Craig Brian Larson (editor), "Illustrations for Preaching and Teaching," *Leadership Journal* (Grand Rapids, MI: Christianity Today, Inc. and Baker Books, a division of Baker Book House Company, 1997), p. 7.

13. C. S. Lewis, *A Grief Observed*, p. 63.

14. Randy Becton, *Everyday Comfort* (Grand Rapids, MI: Baker Books, a division of Baker Book House Company, 1993), p. 64.

15. Elon Foster, *6000 Classic Sermon Illustrations* (Grand Rapids, MI: Baker Book House Company, 1993), p. 753.

16. Craig Brian Larson (editor), "Illustrations for Preaching and Teaching," *Leadership Journal* (Grand Rapids, MI: Christianity Today, Inc. and Baker Books, a division of Baker Book House Company, 1997), p. 114.

17. Elon Foster, *6000 Classic Sermon Illustrations* (Grand Rapids, MI: Baker Book House Company, 1993), p. 346.

18. Craig Brian Larson (editor), "Illustrations for Preaching and Teaching," *Leadership Journal* (Grand Rapids, MI: Christianity Today, Inc. and Baker Books, a division of Baker Book House Company, 1997), p. 12.

19. Dutch Sheets, *Tell Your Heart To Beat Again* (Ventura, CA: Regal Books from Gospel Light, 2002), p. 76

20. Ibid., p. 118.

21. Ibid., p. 72.

22. Ibid., pp. 56, 57.

23. Elon Foster, *6000 Classic Sermon Illustrations* (Grand Rapids, MI: Baker Book House Company, 1993), p. 366.

24. Gerald L. Sittser, *A Grace Disguised* (Grand Rapids, MI: Zondervan Publishing House, 1996), p. 11.

25. Randy Becton, *Everyday Comfort* (Grand Rapids, MI: Baker Books, a division of Baker Book House Company, 1993), p. 42.

26. Ibid., p. 71.

27. Edward K. Rowell (editor), "Fresh Illustrations for Preaching and Teaching," *Leadership Journal* (Grand Rapids, MI: Christianity Today, Inc. and Baker Books, a division of Baker Book House Company, 1997), p. 50.

28. Ibid., p. 203.

29. John M. Drescher (author) in *Pulpit Digest* and Craig Brian Larson (editor), "Illustrations for Preaching and Teaching," *Leadership Journal* (Grand Rapids, MI: Christianity Today, Inc. and Baker Books, a division of Baker Book House Company, 1997), p. 112.

30. Ray Besson and Ranelda Mack Hunsicker (authors) in *The Hidden Price of Greatness* and Edward K. Rowell (editor), *Fresh Illustrations for Preaching and Teaching—from Leadership Journal* (Christianity Today, Inc. and Baker Books a division of Baker Book House Company, 1997), p. 210

Hebrew and Greek
word definitions have been taken from:

1. Spiros Zodhiates, *The Hebrew-Greek Key Study Bible* (Spiros Zodhiates and AMG International, Inc. D/B/A AMG Publishers, 1992), #KE9N.

2. James Strong, *The New Strong's Exhaustive Concordance of the Bible* (Nashville, TN: Thomas Nelson Publishers, 1990), s.v. "matteh," ref. no. 4294.

Contact Information:

To contact Chris Jackson call:

Springs Harvest Fellowship at 719-548-8226.

To contact Dutch Sheets Ministries

Phone: 719-548-8226.

Fax: 719-548-8209.

Email:

ministryinfo@dutchsheets.org

or

www.dutchsheets.org